DATE DUE		

SEAMUS HEANEY

Seamus Heaney

HELEN VENDLER

Harvard University Press
Cambridge, Massachusetts
1998

This edition published by arrangement
with HarperCollins*Publishers* Ltd

Helen Vendler asserts the moral right to
be identified as the author of this work

Set in Postscript Linotype Janson by
Rowland Phototypesetting Ltd,
Bury St Edmunds, Suffolk

Printed in the United States of America

Library of Congress Cataloging-in-Publication Data

Vendler, Helen Hennessy.
Seamus Heaney / Helen Vendler.
      p.   cm.
      ISBN 0-674-79611-x
1. Heaney, Seamus—Criticism and interpretation.
2. Northern Ireland—In literature.   I. Title.
      PR6058.E2Z94   1998
      821'.914—dc21
      98–12413

CONTENTS

For

Bettina Hennessy Pineault   George Hennessy
Joe Pineault   Dorothy Hogan Hennessy

They were my close companions many a year,
A portion of my mind and life, as 'twere.

W. B. YEATS

ACKNOWLEDGEMENTS

I am grateful to Seamus Heaney, first and foremost, for all the invaluable poetry and prose that he has added to the store of literature in English. Over the years, both Seamus and Marie Heaney have courteously provided answers to questions I asked about the poems. Seamus Heaney kindly checked the Chronology of this book and provided the Discography. He has not read this manuscript: any errors remaining are mine alone.

My interest in Irish poetry arose first from a course in Victorian Poetry (including early Yeats) by Professor Morton Berman of Boston University; it was deepened by courses in modern Irish writing given at Harvard University by Professor John V. Kelleher, who directed my dissertation on Yeats and has generously supported my intellectual efforts ever since. I am also indebted to the Yeats Committee and the Directors of the Yeats International Summer School of Sligo, Ireland, where I first heard Seamus Heaney read his work in 1975.

Professor Frank Kermode, General Editor of the Fontana Modern Masters series, commissioned this book, which without him might not have existed in its present form. I am indebted to the editors of the *New York Times Book Review*, the *New York Review of Books*, the *New Yorker*, the *New Republic*, the *Cambridge Review* and the *Harvard Review*, who, by inviting me over the years to write on Heaney's work, have helped me in the preparation for this longer effort, though I do not quote here any of my earlier essays on Heaney. For my opportunity to write on Heaney in my Ellmann Lectures, *The Breaking of Style*, I thank Professor Ronald Schuchard of Emory University. In 1995, as the

Charles Stewart Parnell Lecturer at Magdalene College, Cambridge, I lectured on Heaney in the welcoming atmosphere of the Irish Studies Colloquium, and participated in a public conversation with Seamus Heaney under the auspices of the college, where my kind host was Professor Eamon Duffy.

I am sincerely grateful for the work of the bibliographers, scholars, critics, editors of collections, journalists and interviewers who have discussed Heaney's writing since he first began to publish. They have not only laid the basis for tracking Heaney's allusions, his intellectual and poetic sources, and his development over time; they have also helped to create the terms – literary and political – in which his work has been hitherto discussed. Whether agreeing or disagreeing with them, I have found them serious and stimulating.

The Corporation of Yaddo granted me the Iphigene Ochs Sulzberger Residency for the summer of 1997, when I was engaged in writing this book. My thanks go to the Director of Yaddo, Dr Michael Sundell, and to my Harvard colleague, the poet Henri Cole, who sponsored my visit to Yaddo and thereby gave me an invaluable eight weeks of solitude, comfort and congenial company. The libraries of Harvard University and of Skidmore College have been indispensable to the completion of this book.

I am grateful to Faber & Faber for permission to quote at length from the poetry of Seamus Heaney, and to Farrar, Straus and Giroux for American permissions.

My sister and brother, and my brother-in-law and sister-in-law, named on the dedicatory page, have warmly supported me in my writing, and have been happy for me in the results of that work. I thank them for their life-long affection and encouragement.

CHRONOLOGY

1939:   Born to Patrick Heaney and Margaret
           Kathleen Heaney, 13 April, in County Derry,
           Northern Ireland, at family farm, 'Mossbawn'.
           Eldest of nine children.

1945–51:   Attends Anahorish School, a 'mixed'
           elementary school of Catholic and Protestant
           children. Master Bernard Murphy, who taught
           Latin to Heaney, is commemorated in 'Station
           Island' V.

1947:   Northern Ireland Education Act enables access
           to higher education for children of poorer
           families; it enables Heaney to attend
           St Columb's College in Derry as a boarder on
           scholarship, and, later, to attend Queen's
           University on a 'State Exhibition' bursary.

1951–7:   At St Columb's, where he meets Seamus
           Deane (poet and critic, later to edit the Field
           Day Anthology).

1953:   Younger brother Christopher, four years old,
           killed by car on road near house (recalled in
           poem 'Mid-Term Break').

1956:   Heaney passes A-levels in English, Latin, Irish,
           French and Mathematics with A grades; wins
           bursary to study at Queen's University,
           Belfast.

1957–61:   At Queen's, where he takes First Class
           Honours in English, and is awarded McMullen

Medal for academic achievement. In 1959 first
poems published in Queen's literary magazine.

1961–2: Studies at St Joseph's College of Education,
Belfast, for Teacher's Training Diploma.

1962: Teaches at St Thomas's Intermediate School,
Belfast. Headmaster Michael McLaverty,
fiction writer, is commemorated in 'Singing
School'. Heaney reads the poetry of Patrick
Kavanagh, and undertakes part-time
post-graduate study at Queen's during
1962–3.

1963–6: Teaches at St Joseph's College of Education;
attends Belfast Group meetings led by poet
and Queen's University lecturer Philip
Hobsbaum, where poets (including Michael
Longley and James Simmons) read and
critique each other's work.

1965: Marries Marie Devlin of Ardboe in County
Tyrone, graduate of St Mary's College of
Education in Belfast, 1962.

1966: Son Michael born. *Death of a Naturalist*
published. Heaney becomes lecturer at
Queen's.

1968: Son Christopher (named for dead brother)
born.

1968–9: Catholic civil rights marches, countered by
state police.

1969: *Door into the Dark* published. In August British
troops sent into Belfast and Derry
(commemorated in 'Singing School'). Heaney
spends two months in Europe during the
summer in fulfilment of the requirements of

Somerset Maugham Award.

1970–71: In United States as visiting professor at University of California, Berkeley.

1971: Internment without trial permitted in Northern Ireland.

1972: 30 January: In Derry, 'Bloody Sunday' (so-called in reference to earlier 'Bloody Sunday' of 21 November 1920, when the IRA killed eleven unarmed British officers in Dublin, members of the Dublin Castle Intelligence Unit, and in reprisal the British Army shot 21 members of a crowd watching a football match in Croke Park, Dublin). Paratroopers from the British army kill thirteen unarmed civil rights marchers and wound twelve. Heaney recalls his participation in protest march at Newry, 1972, in 'Triptych' III. The Heaneys move to Glanmore Cottage, near Ashford, County Wicklow, in the Republic of Ireland; cottage (former gate-keeper's cottage on Synge estate) rented to Heaneys by Professor Anne Saddlemeyer, editor of Synge's letters. (Several years later, the Heaneys buy the cottage.) *Wintering Out* published.

1973: Daughter, Catherine Ann, born; event remembered in 'A Pillowed Head'.

1975: *North* published. W. H. Smith Award and Duff Cooper Prize. Heaney begins teaching at Carysfort Teacher Training College, Dublin, where he becomes Head of Department. Friendship with Robert Lowell.

1976:   Heaneys move to Dublin, living near
             Sandymount Strand.

1979:   *Field Work* published. Heaney returns to the
             United States as a visiting professor for one
             term at Harvard University, Cambridge,
             Massachusetts.

1980:   *Preoccupations* (essays and articles) published.
             Poems 1965–1975 published.

1980–81:   Ten Republican prisoners die in hunger strike
             protesting criminal status, claiming political
             status. One (unnamed) appears in 'Station
             Island' IX, perhaps Francis Hughes of
             Bellaghy. Other deaths from sectarian causes
             commemorated in 'Station Island' are those of
             Heaney's cousin Colum McCartney (VIII) and
             Heaney's friend William Strathearn, a
             pharmacist who was murdered in a sectarian
             killing by two off-duty policemen (VII).

1981:   Heaney receives offer of professorship from
             Harvard; resigns from position at Carysfort
             College. Joins Field Day, group founded by
             Brian Friel (playwright) and Stephen Rea
             (actor) to mount theatre in Derry.

1982:   Begins five-year term contract with Harvard,
             teaching one semester per year. Teaching
             includes workshops in creative writing and
             lecture courses in modern poetry, both British
             and Irish.

1983:   Translation of medieval Irish poem *Buile
             Suibhne* published as *Sweeney Astray*. *An Open
             Letter* published as Field Day Pamphlet #2,
             objecting to being included as 'British' in *The*

Penguin Anthology of Contemporary British Poetry, edited by Andrew Motion and Blake Morrison.

1984:   *Station Island* published. Appointed Boylston Professor of Rhetoric and Oratory at Harvard. Margaret Heaney dies, commemorated in 'Clearances'.

1986:   Patrick Heaney dies, commemorated in 'The Stone Verdict'.

1987:   *Haw Lantern* published. Whitbread Award.

1988:   *Government of the Tongue* (essays) published. Elected to five-year term 1989–94 as Professor of Poetry at Oxford, to give three public lectures each year.

1989:   *The Place of Writing* (Richard Ellmann Lectures) published.

1990:   *The Cure at Troy* (a version of Sophocles's *Philoctetes*) published, and performed by Field Day Theatre Company in Derry. *Selected Poems 1966–1987* published.

1991:   *Seeing Things* published.

1994:   Tentative ceasefire in Northern Ireland, commemorated in 'Tollund'.

1995:   10 December: Heaney awarded the Nobel Prize for Literature in Stockholm, Sweden. *The Redress of Poetry* (Oxford lectures) published.

1996:   *The Spirit Level* published. Commonwealth Award. Heaney resigns Boylston Professorship at Harvard, is appointed Emerson Poet in Residence to visit Harvard in non-teaching status every other autumn for six weeks.

1997:   *The Spirit Level* named Whitbread 'Book of
             the Year'. In July, renewed ceasefire in
             Northern Ireland after Labour victory in
             Britain.

ABBREVIATIONS

(See Bibliography for publishing information.)

CP	*Crediting Poetry*
DD	*Door into the Dark*
DN	*Death of a Naturalist*
FW	*Field Work*
GT	*The Government of the Tongue*
HL	*The Haw Lantern*
N	*North*
P	*Preoccupations*
RP	*The Redress of Poetry*
SA	*Sweeney Astray*
SI	*Station Island*
SL	*The Spirit Level*
SP	*Selected Poems 1966–1987*
ST	*Seeing Things*
WO	*Wintering Out*

INTRODUCTION

'Reality is not simply there, it must be sought for and won.'

PAUL CELAN, in answer to a questionnaire from the
Librairie Flinker

In the following pages, I trace Seamus Heaney's development as a poet from 1966 to 1996. It was in 1995 that Heaney (who was born in 1939 in Northern Ireland) was awarded the Nobel Prize for this body of work, composed during what he called, in his Nobel Lecture, 'a quarter century of life waste and spirit waste' (CP, 24). Heaney was referring to daily life in Northern Ireland, disturbed by internal strife since the late 1960s. The Catholic civil rights marches of the sixties (protesting discrimination in jobs and housing, and gerrymandering of political districts), followed by police repression, led to disturbances that the Ulster government attempted to quell in 1971 by the internment without trial of thousands of citizens; in 1972 the (British) army killing of fourteen unarmed Catholic marchers on 'Bloody Sunday' provoked direct rule of Northern Ireland from Westminster. Terrorist actions on the part of both the Provisional IRA and the Ulster paramilitaries escalated, and – though motions towards a cessation of violence have been put forward since 1994, a permanent ceasefire is not yet securely in place. These conditions forced Heaney (who had been raised a Catholic) into becoming a poet of public as well as private life.

Heaney's poetry has reached a large public in Ireland and abroad, and that public extends to all classes. It is a poetry in which readers can recognize profound family affections, eloquent landscapes, and vigorous social concern. It tells an expressive autobiographical story reaching from boyhood to Heaney's present age of sixty, a story which includes a childhood at home with parents, relatives, siblings; an adolescence with schoolfellows and friends; an adulthood with a marriage and children; a displacement from Northern Ireland to the Republic; travels; sorrows and deaths. As each decade of poetry unfolds, it illuminates and corrects the previous ones. Within its autobiographical circuit, it is also an oeuvre of strong social engagement, looking steadily and with stunning poetic force at what it means to be a contemporary citizen of Northern Ireland – at the intolerable stresses put on the population by conflict, fear, betrayals, murders. Heaney has made one imaginative cast after another in an attempt to represent the almost unrepresentable collective suffering of the North, yet he has tried, equally consistently, to bring intellectual reflection to the emotional attitudes that too often yield the binary position-taking of propaganda.

These would seem to be the achievements of Heaney's poetry; and most of his readers, if asked, would cite the autobiographical and the political as aspects drawing them to his poems. But these thematic elements do not by themselves make for memorable poetry, and the powerful symbols Heaney has found for his poetry are responsible for much of its effect. His commentators find themselves talking not merely of but within those powerful symbols – the exhumed bog bodies in *North*, the Lough Derg pilgrims in *Station Island*, the political parables of frontiers and islands in *The Haw Lantern*. Heaney has made out of his symbols a shorthand for his era. Yet even adequately-imagined symbols do not suffice for memorable work: poetry needs words and syntax as strikingly expressive as its themes and its symbols, and it also requires internal structures that 'act out' the emotions they exist to convey. Heaney's language is unusually rich in simplicity as well as in ornateness, each where it suits; his syntax is sinuous and expressive, whether it is sternly terse or restlessly mobile; and his highly-developed sense of internal structure gives his poems a satisfying musical 'rightness' as they unfold. Each of his volumes ambitiously sets itself a different task from its predecessors; each takes up a new form of writing; and just when one thinks one knows all of Heaney's possibilities of style, he unfurls a new one. His readers, even when they do not notice technique in any explicit way, are being persuaded into the poem by words, by syntax, by structures, as well as by themes and symbols. 'Feeling into Words', the title of an early essay by Heaney, can be taken as the motto for all his work.

My own acquaintance with Heaney's work began in 1975. I was lecturing at the Yeats School in Sligo in the summer of that year, and at the school's annual poetry reading a young man in his thirties named Seamus Heaney, wholly unknown to me, stood at the lectern and read some of the most extraordinary poems I had ever heard. I approached him afterwards, and asked whether these poems were to appear soon in a book as I wanted to write about them. Heaney replied that in fact he had galleys with him, and lent them to me. They were the galleys of *North*, which I thought then – and still think now – one of the crucial poetic interventions of the twentieth century, ranking with *Prufrock* and *Harmonium* and *North of Boston* in its key role in the history of modern poetry.

I reviewed *North* for the *New York Times Book Review* a few months later, and have been writing about Heaney ever since. My startled and wholehearted response on first encountering Heaney's writing was by no means unique: his poetry has now been translated and appreciated all over the world, and the Nobel is only one of several foreign prizes (in addition to many from English-speaking countries) awarded to his work. The purpose of this book is to explain, as much to myself as to others, the power of his extraordinary poetry. It derives – as all poetry does – from the inspiration of predecessors, and the most important of these for Heaney have been (in the English/Irish/American tradition) the *Beowulf*-poet, the anonymous author of the Middle Irish poem *Buile Suibhne*, William Wordsworth, John Keats, Gerard Manley Hopkins, W. B. Yeats, James Joyce, Robert Frost, Patrick Kavanagh and Ted Hughes. Among classical poets, one should mention Aeschylus and Virgil; among foreign poets, Dante, Osip Mandelstam and Zbigniew Herbert. Heaney has written about many of these authors in his essays on poetry; and scholars have begun to trace specific instances of intertextual connections in Heaney's poetry. I cannot – for reasons of space – treat influence here, but Heaney is among the most learned of contemporary poets, and has brought together influences not often found conjoined in creating his own unmistakable style.

Nor can I describe, here, the generational context in which Heaney appears, though I can at least list a portion of it, giving the more celebrated names. Heaney was preceded by John Hewitt, John Montague and Thomas Kinsella, and fellowed by Seamus Deane, Michael Longley and Derek Mahon. He has been followed by (among others) Tom Paulin, Paul Muldoon, Medbh McGuckian and Ciaran Carson. Each of these poets – some Protestant, some Catholic, some Northern, some Southern – has brought a distinctive voice to the second half of the twentieth century in Ireland; each has also been part of a new wave of Irish writing of linguistic variety and imaginative depth. Literary historians have already begun to chart this period, and literary critics to dispute positions concerning it. Heaney's influence on his successors has been almost as intimidating as Yeats's influence on those coming after him; but successful flanking motions have been invented in Paulin's grittiness of surface, Muldoon's enigmatic comedy, McGuckian's stream-of-consciousness imagery, and Ciaran Carson's long urban line.

The author of lyric – as my epigraph from Paul Celan implies – is obliged to search out, for any given situation, a symbolic plane on which to represent both reality, as he perceives it to be, and his responses to it. Historically, from the Greek Anthology to Palgrave's *Golden Treasury*, lyric has been seen to occupy itself chiefly with the private life. But Heaney (like Milton, Wordsworth and Yeats) could not escape the political convulsions of his place and time, and his lyrics soon took on colour from the centuries-old difficulties of the North – great and intractable problems of long standing, which have been variously analysed as differences of religious affiliation (Catholic versus Protestant), of political affiliation (Nationalist versus Unionist), of class (the deprived versus the economically dominant), of region (the agricultural against the industrial), and of tribe (Celts versus Anglo-Saxons). Though in 1972 Heaney and his family left Belfast (and its repeated riots and murders) for the Republic of Ireland, the North has never ceased to shadow his work, for all his deliberate (and often brilliantly successful) poems on other subjects. In his writing, the public and the private compete for space, and the tragic and the quotidian contest each other's dominance.

As Heaney put it in his Nobel Lecture, his writing, like his life, has been 'a journey where each point of arrival . . . turned out to be a stepping-stone rather than a destination' (CP, 9). I have treated his individual volumes as stepping-stones in the narrative that follows, but I have included only so much of the life as is necessary to my commentary on the poems.[1] I have not treated Heaney's vivid, metaphorical and intelligent prose – *Preoccupations* (1980), *The Government of the Tongue* (1988), *The Place of Writing* (1989), *The Redress of Poetry* (1995) and the Nobel Lecture *Crediting Poetry* (1996) – because to do so would exceed the length allowed for this volume; for the same reason I have not commented on *The Cure at Troy*, his translation of Sophocles' *Philoctetes* (1991).

Nor have I taken issue here with Heaney's negative critics. The terms of reproof against Heaney have been almost entirely thematic. Some feminists regret in the poetry an absence of women engaged in other than domestic roles, and have detected 'patriarchal' attitudes in the poet. Some political journalists denounce Heaney for not making more outspokenly partisan statements for 'his side'; others argue that though he overtly deplores violence, in fact his poetry covertly supports Republican attitudes. (I myself regard thematic arguments about poetry as beside the point. Lyric poetry neither stands nor falls on its themes; it stands or falls on the accuracy of language with which it reports the author's emotional responses to the life around him.) Most of the longer books mentioned in the appended *Bibliography* offer a survey of critical reactions to Heaney's work, including negative ones. It goes without saying, perhaps, that the response to his poetry on the part of general readers and literary critics – in Ireland, the United Kingdom, the United States and Europe – has been overwhelmingly positive. I want here chiefly to show by what imaginative, structural and stylistic means Heaney raises his subjects to a plane that compels such worldwide admiration.

Once the poet has found the symbolic plane on which to sketch his topic – as, say, Keats was able to contemplate the rivalry to poetry offered by the visual arts and music by sketching the former through the Grecian urn and the latter through the nightingale – he must find a way (since poetry is a temporal art) to prolong that symbolic plane through time. This need to prolong creates the structure of the poem (which may be sequential, contrastive, dialogic, climactic, etc.); this temporal structure itself must, in a poem of the first order, be formally expressive of the symbolic theme. (That is, a poem contrasting two states could be written in two contrasting stanzas – as is the case in 'A Slumber Did My Spirit Seal' – or in the octave-sestet contrast of a sonnet, or in any other form, such as a dialogue, that supported its contrastive theme.)

Beyond the chosen symbolic plane and its prolongation in a formally supportive temporal architectonic plan the poet must find the right 'dictionary', syntax and sensory focus for his subject. Will its lexicon be Latinate or Anglo-Saxon in 'feel'? Will its grammar be simple and rustic, or learned and complex? Will it be a visual landscape-like poem or an 'auditory' poem full of sounds and colloquy? (These are merely instances: a poem can be 'French' or 'Chinese' in feel, instead of 'Latinate' or 'Anglo-Saxon'; a poem can move, as Keats's 'To Autumn' does, from the visual to the auditory, or vice versa.) And finally the poet must find his own persona and tonal stance within his material: will he appear as his historical self or as a generalized lyric speaker? Will he speak 'objectively' or from an identifiable political or social position?

Each successful poem presents itself as a unique experiment in language. The experiment of one can never be repeated in another; each, as Keats said in an 1818 letter to his publisher John Taylor, is 'a regular stepping of the Imagination toward a Truth'.[2] Keats's use of the indefinite article – 'a Truth' – indicates the provisional nature of all lyric compositions. Each poem says, 'Viewed from this angle, at this moment, in this year, with this focus, the subject appears to me in this light, and my responses to it spring from this set of feelings.' Since no lyric can be equal to the whole complexity of private and public life at any given moment, lyrics are not to be read as position papers.

Rather, they are a screen on which one can read the patterns
of the nerves on a given day (as Eliot justly said in 'The
Waste Land'). When Heaney speaks (in his essay 'Feeling
into Words') of his first attempts as a poet, he says, 'I was
in love with words themselves, but had no sense of a poem
as a whole structure and no experience of how the successful
achievement of a poem could be a stepping stone in your
life' (P, 45). It was only later that he learned what must be
added to the love of words in order to make a poem, a
quality he calls 'technique':

> Technique, as I would define it, involves not only
> a poet's way with words, his management of metre,
> rhythm and verbal texture; it involves also a defi-
> nition of his stance towards life. . . . It involves . . .
> a dynamic alertness that mediates between the
> origins of feeling in memory and experience and
> the formal ploys that express these in a work of
> art. . . . It is that whole creative effort . . . to bring
> the meaning of experience within the jurisdiction
> of form.
>
>   [P, 47]

The 'jurisdiction of form' is different for each poem: 'You
are confirmed', Heaney adds, 'by the visitation of the last
poem and threatened by the elusiveness of the next one' (P,
54).

All this was true before the riots of 1969 in Derry (I
follow Heaney's usage of this name) and Belfast, but the
political upheavals of that summer changed Heaney's fundamental aim as a poet: 'From that moment the problems of
poetry moved from being simply a matter of achieving the
satisfactory verbal icon to being a search for images and
symbols adequate to our predicament' (P, 56). The plurals
in this statement must be emphasized: the historical predica-

ment demands that the poet 'search' and 'win' reality –
Celan's words quoted in my epigraph – through *many*
images (local metaphors) and *many* symbols (whole-poem
symbolic structures), no one of which can possibly have total
spatial or temporal or imaginative adequacy to public and
private history. It is for this reason that each poem can only
be one of many stepping-stones, and why each can only
point towards – rather than achieve – 'a' truth. At the same
time, in being faithful to his subject, his feelings and his
symbolic forms, the poet cannot forget the rich texture of
language proper to lyric, that phonological 'binding secret',
as Heaney has called it (P, 186), which makes the utterance
seem something that could not be said in any other set of
words.

Heaney's adversary critics read the poems as statements
of a political position, with which they quarrel. To read
lyric poems as if they were expository essays is a fundamental
philosophical mistake; and part of the purpose of this book
is to read the poems as the provisional symbolic structures
that they are. Naturally, not all of Heaney's symbolic force-
fields can be equally well realized; every poet is uneven, and
any single volume will be uneven. None the less, the aesthetic and intellectual experiment attempted in each Heaney
poem is a serious one. Because a reflective poet, as he ages,
incorporates his past into his present, the existential burden
on his more ambitious lyrics becomes heavier over time.
Ideally, a lyric of large scope – 'Lycidas' or 'Nineteen Hundred and Nineteen' or 'The Waste Land' – wants to leave its
reader feeling that nothing has been left out, that everything
relevant to the current situation and the speaker's response
to it has been brought into expression. Heaney's sequences
– from the 1975 'Singing School' to the 1996 'Mycenae
Lookout' – attempt, by a series of symbolic purchases, to
gain a larger, though still partial, hold on the present and
past together. I admire this attempt to be comprehensive

while not betraying the fundamental aim of lyric: to grasp and perpetuate, by symbolic form, the self's volatile and transient here and now.

In the pages that follow I take up in detail some of Heaney's strongest poems to show the lyric process in action, and to investigate how form becomes realized in words. 'To hold in a single thought reality and justice' – Yeats's definition in *A Vision* of the hope of lyric – is one that Heaney has often quoted. Reality is how things are; justice is how things should be. Because one's sense of both reality and justice changes over time, Heaney is a writer especially given, as he says in 'Terminus', to 'second thoughts'.

> Two buckets were easier carried than one.
> I grew up in between.
>
> My left hand placed the standard iron weight.
> My right tilted a last grain in the balance.
>
> Baronies, parishes met where I was born.
>
> [HL, 5]

'Is it any wonder,' he comments, that 'when I thought / I would have second thoughts?' As his intellectual and moral horizons widen, Heaney's 'second thoughts' become fundamental to his development, so much so that I have appended to each chapter, under the heading 'Second Thoughts', a foretaste of how Heaney will write, later in life, about the concerns taken up in that chapter. Heaney's prose shows similar changes over time. Though fundamental aspects of his thought remain – the abiding anxiety over the social function of poetry, for instance, or the quarrel between aesthetic form and moral urgency – the metaphors in which he embodies such worries do alter from essay to essay, from poem to poem. It is for this reason that quoting a sentence or a stanza from Heaney and adducing that it gives 'his opinion' on this or that political question betrays the fluidity and responsiveness of his mind. I have tried here, above all, to be faithful to his vigilant willingness to change.

In the title essay of *The Government of the Tongue* Heaney makes his single most profound statement on the social function of writing in a moment of human extremity. He borrows an image from the gospel of John, that of Jesus writing in the sand when confronting the accusers of the woman taken in adultery. Heaney says:

> In one sense the efficacy of poetry is nil – no lyric has ever stopped a tank. In another sense, it is unlimited. It is like the writing in the sand in the face of which accusers and accused are left speechless and renewed.
>
> I am thinking of Jesus' writing as it is recorded in Chapter Eight of John's Gospel [in which Jesus twice, in answer to the hectoring scribes and Pharisees, bends silently and writes with his finger on the ground; the evangelist does not say what he writes, but the writing – in addition to Jesus' answer, 'He that is without sin among you, let him first cast a stone at her' – leads the crowd, 'convicted by their own conscience', to depart].
>
> The drawing of those characters is like poetry, a break with the usual life but not an absconding from it. Poetry, like the writing, is arbitrary and marks time in every possible sense of that phrase. It does not say to the accusing crowd or to the helpless accused, 'Now a solution will take place', it does not propose to be instrumental or effective. Instead, in the rift between what is going to happen

and whatever we would wish to happen, poetry
holds attention for a space, functions not as distraction but as pure concentration, a focus where our
power to concentrate is concentrated back on ourselves.

[GT, 107–8]

Heaney's emphasis here is that of lyric: 'a focus where our
power to concentrate is concentrated back on ourselves'.
Lyric is not narrative or drama; it is not primarily concerned
to relate events, or to reify contesting issues. Rather, its act
is to present, adequately and truthfully, through the means
of temporally prolonged symbolic form, the private mind
and heart caught in the changing events of a geographical
place and a historical epoch. Heaney's lyrics – as the chapters
that follow will, I hope, convey – have done that for himself,
his country and his time, while enlarging the specifically
literary inheritance on which they depend. He has rethought
the sonnet, the elegy, the historical poem, the archaeological
poem, the sequence; he has invented a new vein of pheno-
menological abstraction in landscape poetry; he has renovated terza rima in demotic language, and, in his 'squarings',
explored the potential of the douzain. He has written with
an acute sense of the linguistic inheritances, both etymological and syntactic, of English – from Anglo-Saxon, Latin,
the Romance languages – and has renovated the English of
Irish poetry in consequence. Poems become memorable if,
and only if, they renovate language and symbol and structure
and genre; otherwise they fall into the abyss of the forgotten.
Though I have attempted to make fair summaries of
Heaney's intentions in the commentaries that follow, I have
tried to point out, too, how each poem makes itself distinctive and striking. (All page references following citations of
poetry are to the first Faber edition of that volume.)

1

Anonymities:
Death of a Naturalist,
Door into the Dark, Wintering Out

> Under the broom . . .
> Yellowing over them, compose the frieze
> With all of us there, our anonymities.
>
> 'The Seed Cutters' (N, xi)

> From being a frieze of symbolic figures representative
> of the matter of Ireland, Clarke's poetry became a
> series of rapid probes and sketches which were symp-
> tomatic of what was the matter with Ireland.
>
> SEAMUS HEANEY, 'A tale of two islands:
> reflections on the Irish Literary Revival'[3]

To move from 'the matter of Ireland' to 'what was the
matter with Ireland' – Heaney's summary of the change in
the poetry of Austin Clarke – could as well describe his own
development. In Heaney's early work 'symbolic figures',
such as those in 'The Seed Cutters', stand for the poet's
recognition of the immemorial nature of the work done
on the family farm, which he is intent on perpetuating in
language. Because such figures are anonymous, his poetic
voice will also be anonymous: he will speak both about and
for those whose names are lost to history.

The particularity conferred by one's proper name is of
interest to Heaney, too, and will play its role in his poetry
when he turns from anonymity to historic specificity – writ-

ing as an adult man of a particular place in a particular time. But his child-self is almost anonymous, and many of the poems of childhood treat (in ample and beautiful ways) experiences that could be those of any child growing up on a farm and watching the daily and seasonal rituals such as churning or haymaking. Through his childhood recollections, Heaney attains an almost anonymous manner, and these recollections form the central group of his first two books, *Death of a Naturalist* (1966) and *Door into the Dark* (1969). Yet anonymity is not usually the first choice of a young poet, and to comprehend this initial choice of writerly identity we might enquire what Heaney's other choices of identity as a speaker might have been.

Those who grow up with an awareness of words very soon tabulate the anonymous group-names under which others denominate them – in Heaney's case, 'Catholics', 'farmers', 'Northern Irish'. These group-names exist beyond one's first, familial, child-name ('Seamus'); beyond the family name ('the Heaneys'); beyond one's surname in formal use at school ('Heaney'). Heaney's poetry notes each of these identities as it is inscribed. As the child hides in the hollow trunk of a tree, he hears the family calling his first name, seeking him out:

> Hide in the hollow trunk
> of the willow tree,
> its listening familiar,
> until, as usual, they
> cuckoo your name
> across the fields.
> You can hear them
> draw the poles of stiles
> as they approach
> calling you out.

The family summons, announcing the claims of home, disturbs the child's anonymous crouching in the 'secret nest' of nature ('Mossbawn', P, 17), where he is more a tree-spirit than a human child: he becomes a

> small mouth and ear
> in a woody cleft,
> lobe and larynx
> of the mossy places.

['Oracle', WO, 28]

In a later poem, 'Alphabets', the child's recognition that he is more than 'Seamus', that he is one of a circle of kin sharing his surname, closes the narrative: after the plastering of his childhood house is finished the boy, not yet of school age, watches with a

> wide pre-reflective stare
> All agog at the plasterer on his ladder
> Skimming our gable and writing our name there
> With his trowel point, letter by strange letter.

['Alphabets', HL, 3]

Still later, in secondary school, there is a moment of adolescent confusion when a priest asks the boy-student (normally called 'Heaney') what his name is (meaning his first name): the boy, flustered, replies automatically, and receives in turn a wry acknowledgement:

> 'What's your name, Heaney?'
>   'Heaney, Father.'
>   'Fair
> Enough.'

[N, 58]

Then, as a young university student, heading home in his car after an evening out with a girl, the poet is stopped and interrogated by police at a road-block. He gives his personal and familial name instead of the full name expected by the police who, in reply, challenge him:

>   policemen
> Swung their crimson flashlamps, crowding round
> The car like black cattle, snuffing and pointing
> The muzzle of a sten-gun in my eye:
> 'What's your name, driver?'
>   'Seamus . . .'
>   *Seamus?*

['Singing School', I, N, 58]

The police in Ulster, normally Protestant, were not friendly to anyone with the 'Catholic' name of Seamus (the Irish version of 'James'), but the innocence of the poet's reply shows that he still identifies himself as the person his friends and family know.

All these identities, and more, enter into the voice that becomes that of a poet. How, then, should the poet write? As a child and family member ('Seamus')? As an individual adult with a singular identity ('Seamus Heaney')? Or should he write more anonymously: as a representative of the rural (by contrast to the urban) population? As someone who is culturally Irish, attached to a historical and anthropological identity that predates, in its beginnings, the Christianization of the country? Or as a 'Catholic', a spokesperson for an ethnic group sharing a certain culture (of which one strand is the childhood practice of Catholicism that may well be abandoned in adult life)? As an English speaker, reader and writer? Or as a transmitter of an Irish literary tradition? Perhaps as a European, or even (like Yeats in his latter years) as a world poet? Or, rather, should the poet be content to write as an anonymous moral perceiver – setting aside, as far as possible, the local ideological assumptions acquired through family and education? These are – as Heaney said in the Foreword to the 1980 *Preoccupations*, his first collection of essays – central questions: 'How should a poet properly live and write? What is his relationship to be to his own voice, his own place, his literary heritage and his contemporary world?' (P, 11) Yet Heaney knew that such questions could not be answered by looking to the opinions of others: he made that clear by quoting, as epigraph to those early essays, the following sentences, written by Yeats in 1905:

> If I had written to convince others I would have asked myself, not 'Is that exactly what I think and feel?' but 'How would that strike so-and-so? How will they think and feel when they have read it?' And all would be oratorical and insincere. If we understand our own minds, and the things that are striving to utter themselves through our minds, we move others, not because we have understood or thought about those others, but because all life has the same root.
>
> [P, 14]

If, then, Heaney is to write about any of the several groups to which he belongs (or to which he is assigned by others), he vows not to be intimidated by what those groups think of him and his work – what the priests might want to find; what the relatives may say; what Ulster Protestants would approve; what fellow-poets hope to hear; what predecessors advise. This vow is one all poets must take, and one which is always very difficult to keep; but it becomes particularly hard when the claims of affection and solidarity attempt to establish confines around what can be said and written. The first lecture in Heaney's 1995 collection of essays, *The Redress of Poetry*, contemplates those pressures, weighted by the events of 'Bloody Sunday' in January of 1972; but for the moment we are in the 1960s, the 'Troubles' have not yet reached their 1972 exacerbations, and Heaney has written two books: *Death of a Naturalist* and *Door into the Dark*, which I am treating as his books of 'anonymities'.

The way of life of his father's rural family, as Heaney has remarked, differed little from medieval custom: and in 'Anahorish' his neighbours become indistinguishable from their Neolithic ancestors:

> With pails and barrows
>
> those mound-dwellers
> go waist-deep in mist
> to break the light ice
> at wells and dunghills.
>
> [WO, 16]

One has, of course, already moved far away from one's family if one can see them as 'those mound-dwellers'; and Heaney's commemorative lyrics on the longstanding farm-practices of his family, his neighbours and his ancestors (hand scything; digging potatoes; dealing at cattle fairs; retting flax in a flax dam; thatching; churning; carrying water from a pump shared by several families) are testaments to his first, preservational instincts. He makes himself into an anthropologist of his own culture, and testifies, in each poem, to his profound attachment to the practice described while not concealing his present detachment from rural life. The early 'poems of anonymity' are always elegiac: Heaney will not write from 'inside' or from a present-tense perspective, as though he were still living in the archaic culture he describes.

The eloquent poem 'Thatcher' – which I will take as my example of functional anonymity, though 'The Seed Cutters' or 'The Forge' would do as well – begins as though the coming of the thatcher were an ordinary affair (as indeed it was, when his work was part of the usual maintenance of a house):

> Bespoke for weeks, he turned up some morning
> Unexpectedly, his bicycle slung
> With a light ladder and a bag of knives.
> He eyed the old rigging, poked at the eaves,
> Opened and handled sheaves of lashed wheat-straw.

Everything in this stanza might be said by any one of the inhabitants of the cottage. But by the last stanza Heaney's 'outsideness' is quietly present in the closing reference to 'them' – not 'us'. It is also present in the 'educated' vocabulary (of heraldry in 'couchant', of mythology in 'Midas') that the poet brings to bear in order to exalt the medieval form of the thatcher, and in the Keatsian metaphorical turn ('honeycomb', 'stubble patch') by which he gathers the thatched roof into the storehouse of English pastoral:

> Couchant for days on sods above the rafters,
> He shaved and flushed the butts, stitched all together
> Into a sloped honeycomb, a stubble patch,
> And left them gaping at his Midas touch.

> [DD, 20]

For the reader who notices literary form, the 'outsideness' is already present in Heaney's choice here of the stately pentameter quatrain – a variant (in its rhymed couplets) of the alternately rhymed stanza known in prosody as the 'heroic quatrain'. Such a ceremonious stanza helps to monumentalize the thatcher into a lone survivor from the artisanal days of the guilds. Like the ploughman, the black-smith, the eel-fishers in 'A Lough Neagh Sequence', or the family thawing the frozen pump by setting ropes of wheatstraw aflame ('Rite of Spring'), the thatcher does not realize his own imminent obsolescence. But Heaney does: and though one of these poems ('The Wife's Tale') is Breughelesque in its portrayal of the threshers taking their midday meal in the fields, the presence of a threshing-machine brings the industrial world into this scene, which otherwise might be drawn from a medieval book of hours.

By choosing as his subject anonymous rural labourers, the young poet erects a memorial to the generations of forgotten men and women whose names are lost, whose graves bear no tombstones, and whose lives are registered in no chronicle. Soon even the tools they used will be found only in museums, and the movements they made in wielding them will be utterly lost. It is immensely important to Heaney to note down those expert movements – like an anthropologist inventing a notation for an unrecorded dance – lest they vanish unregistered. So in 'Follower' his father at the plough is described moment by moment, with a piety not only filial but generational:

> My father worked with a horse-plough,
> His shoulders globed like a full sail strung
> Between the shafts and the furrow.
> The horses strained at his clicking tongue.
>
> An expert. He would set the wing
> And fit the bright steel-pointed sock.
> The sod rolled over without breaking.
> At the headrig, with a single pluck

Of reins, the sweating team turned round
And back into the land. His eye
Narrowed and angled at the ground,
Mapping the furrow exactly.

[DN, 12]

Heaney is not uncritical of rural life. Potato-diggers are
followed as they pass by on a headland, gathering the crop
as they go: 'Processional stooping through the turf / Recurs
mindlessly as autumn' ('At a Potato Digging', DN, 18).
Here and in 'Follower', as in 'Thatcher', each vignette of
anonymous labour has its distancing moment: 'I wanted to
grow up and plough,' says the adult poet remembering his
child-self: and the characterization of the potato-diggers'
movement as a pre-ordained 'processional' liturgy, coupled
with the critique of its 'mindless' recurrence, makes that
poem too an elegiac one, representing a life which the poet
does not want to follow, could not follow, but none the less
recognizes as forever a part of his inner landscape.

If writing about labourers engaged in archaic occupations
is one way for a modern poet to submerge his own adult
identity in anonymity, another way is to leave his own historical moment, to speak as an 'I' or a 'we' from another era.
Heaney's early political poem, 'Requiem for the Croppies',
offers in its title a reply to Geoffrey Hill's 'Requiem for
the Plantagenet Kings'. It imagines that the Croppies –
crop-haired Irish footsoldiers of 1798, carrying their food
in their pockets, who were killed by the English army at
the battle of Vinegar Hill in County Wexford – can posthumously speak out to tell their tale. Though the poem has
been called (by Neil Corcoran) a 'dramatic monologue', it
does not take the characteristically social form of the Brown-
ing monologue (which is always addressed to one or more
people in the same room as its living speaker). Heaney's

poem is, rather, a self-epitaph by the Croppies, spoken to anyone who has ears to hear:

> The pockets of our greatcoats full of barley –
> No kitchens on the run, no striking camp –
> We moved quick and sudden in our own country.

The Croppies die 'shaking scythes at cannon': 'They buried us without shroud or coffin / And in August the barley grew up out of the grave' (DD, 24). The resurrection-motif makes the Croppies resemble a vegetation-god. The poet's piety writes for them – creates for them to speak – the epitaph that their lack of funeral rites or a gravestone denied them.

'Requiem for the Croppies' is an anomalous sonnet, adding to its three Shakespearean quatrains a couplet that prolongs the rhymes of the last quatrain instead of introducing a new rhyme-sound: *ababcdcdefefef*. Heaney's surprising choice of the sonnet – that European court form – for his epitaph for an Irish peasant army has formal meaning: it affirms that the old aristocratic genres have life in them yet, and may be translated into poems defending rural values. (Heaney's experimentation with the sonnet continues throughout his writing life.)

Perhaps the most usual way poets devise to be anonymous is to turn to myth and legend (whether classical, Christian or folk-derived), and Heaney takes this path as well. In a rather self-conscious early poem called 'Undine' he writes in the voice of the water-nymph as she recollects her liberation from the earth by the man who 'slashed the briars, shovelled up grey silt / To give me right of way in my own drains' (DD, 26). Though the sexual analogy becomes strained ('He dug a spade deep in my flank / And took me to him. I swallowed his trench'), the poem announces Heaney's interest in assuming (as in 'The Wife's Tale', 'Mother', 'Limbo', 'Shore Woman' and elsewhere) a special type of anonymity:

what it might mean to imagine oneself inside a woman's experience. In this regard, Heaney makes use of folktale as well, summoning up the legend of the capture of a mermaid ('Maighdean Mara') to account for a woman's suicide. Christian legend also attracts Heaney, and in his retelling of St Francis's sermon to the birds, he announces, by describing Francis's means, an aspect of his own literary resolve: 'His argument true, his tone light' ('St Francis and the Birds', DN, 40). The gods, goddesses, nymphs and naiads of classical pastoral do not, finally, become useful to Heaney; and he does not make a practice of writing from within a female sensibility. But he will eventually make notable use – in writing 'anonymously' – of Greek and Latin historical myth (Mycenae; Romulus and Remus) in *The Spirit Level* (1996).

And still another form of anonymity can be gained when the poet becomes wholly a perceptual observer – one with no history, no ethnicity, no religion, no family. This is the form of anonymity that Heaney has, in the long run, found most rewarding. It shows up early in 'The Peninsula'. More than a sonnet, less than a narrative, this important poem (written in four irregular quatrains with embraced rhymes) is chiefly a meditation on the purifying power, for human beings, of the primary senses and of memory founded in the senses. It deserves to be quoted in full as an example of Heaney's early reliance on the perceptual as a never-to-be-forgotten standard of veracity and plain speech. The poem has three parts: the first, a day's drive around the peninsula; the second, the night drive returning home remembering the day's sights; the third, a vow taken. The motive for the drive is writer's block, perhaps a symptom of emotional distress or fear:

The Peninsula

When you have nothing to say, just drive
For a day all round the peninsula.
The sky is tall as over a runway,
The land without marks so you will not arrive

But pass through, though always skirting landfall.
At dusk, horizons drink down sea and hill,
The ploughed field swallows the whitewashed gable
And you're in the dark again. Now recall

The glazed foreshore and silhouetted log,
That rock where breakers shredded into rags,
The leggy birds stilted on their own legs,
Islands riding themselves out into the fog

And drive back home, still with nothing to say
Except that now you will uncode all landscapes
By this: things founded clean on their own shapes,
Water and ground in their extremity.

[DD, 21]

The first scanning of the peninsula is very general (a
'tall' sky, a land 'without marks', sea, hill, ploughed field,
whitewashed cottage). On the dark drive home, the poet
takes an inventory of what he has (perhaps unconsciously)
internally registered as significant. *How did the foreshore look?*
As if it had been glazed – luminous, smooth. *What broke the
horizon line?* A silhouetted log, out of place, far from where
it fell. *What did the breakers look like?* Like a bolt of white
cloth being shredded into rags by the rock. *And what was
strange about the way the sea-birds walked?* They moved with
the awkward gait of one on stilts – but their stilts are their

own legs. And, finally, *How did the island appear when the fog moved in?* The swirl of fog made the offshore islands seem to move of their own volition out into the ocean. That is the driver's visual and mental and emotional harvest – what won't be lost of the day's experience. This reservoir of images that struck home (as we know because they called up metaphors for themselves – glazing, a profiled silhouette, rags, stilts, riding) is a treasury of 'things founded clean on their own shapes'. But it is not solely this lesson of exactness that the poet takes home with him from perceptions brought to clear outline and emotionally inscribed: it is also the lesson of peninsular remoteness, where water and ground meet in their outermost reach, without distraction.

I will be emphasizing, throughout this book, Heaney's recourse to 'second thoughts', and this is an occasion when they can be clearly seen, since Heaney much later 'rewrites' 'The Peninsula' in 'Postscript', the poem that closes *The Spirit Level* (1996). 'Postscript' is another sixteen-line image of a drive, this time 'out west / Into County Clare, along the Flaggy Shore'. It is not writer's block that now afflicts the poet, but rather the tendency of the preoccupied middle-aged heart to shield itself against feeling. Heaney here gratefully pays homage to the sheer power of perception itself – how much it sees in a glimpse, in a glance – how many objects and shades it absorbs at once, how breathtaking the conjunction of world and senses can be, breaking open the shut door of the heart. The poem is perhaps a distant descendant of Hopkins's 'Hurrahing in Harvest':

> These things, these things were here and but the
>   beholder
> Wánting; whích two, whén they ónce méet,
> The héart réars wíngs bóld and bolder,
> And hurls for him, oh half hurls earth for him off
>   under his feet.

But Heaney's poem, caught between the rush of a moment's pure visual satisfaction and the frustration of its transience, goes beyond the ecstatic to a definition of selfhood so fugitive as to be insubstantial. The self is 'a hurry through which ... things pass', nothing more. Itself unfounded, it can hardly hope to 'found things' in the way the younger self thought to do.

The ecstatic moment in 'Postscript', like that in 'Peninsula', is made up of simple components: wind, light, ocean, an inland lake, stones and swans. (In a nod to Yeats's Coole, Heaney rhymes 'stones' and 'swans', but his swans are not paired, 'lover by lover', as Yeats's were: they are, if beautiful, also communal and practical.) Every day at this shore there is wind, light, ocean, the lake, the swans. But not every day do they lap into synergy, as they do at this moment,

> when the wind
> And the light are working off each other
> So that the ocean on one side is wild
> With foam and glitter, and inland among stones
> The surface of a slate-grey lake is lit
> By the earthed lightning of a flock of swans,
> Their feathers roughed and ruffling, white on white,
> Their fully grown headstrong-looking heads
> Tucked or cresting or busy underwater.

This passage could serve as an index to Heaney's sensibility in his fifties. The wild is not forsaken, but it is, like the swans, sometimes 'earthed'. The beautiful is no more alien to the poet than it ever was, but the ordinary must also play its role: the swans are 'headstrong' and 'busy'. The best moments of all are the ones when the wild and the settled parts of being do not forget each other, when the ocean is the partner of the lake, and when wind and light, strength and clarity, contest for presence. (I have allegorized for explicitness; but the poem itself refrains from allegorizing, and keeps the illusion of reportage.)

And then the ecstatic moment is gone; or you are gone; and nothing is retrievable: 'Useless to think you'll park and capture it / More thoroughly.' But the precious sensation of full receptivity has returned for an unforgettable instant in which one's heart has been again as open to feeling as it was in youth:

> You are neither here nor there,
> A hurry through which known and strange things pass
> As big soft buffetings come at the car sideways
> And catch the heart off guard and blow it open.

> [SL, 70]

Perhaps the one thing that all human beings have in common is sense-perception: and there are many shores around the world where such buffetings of wind and light can be experienced. There is no way of knowing whether the author of this poem is male or female, old or young, Catholic or Protestant, Northern or Southern Irish, a city-dweller or a country-dweller. This form of anonymity – in which elusive states of feeling are caught in a descriptive gestalt which powerfully renders them available to others – is one often practised by Wordsworth, whose example can be felt in Heaney, though the Wordsworthian legacy has been powerfully altered through Heaney's deliberately casual and modern diction.

In his early work even the personal Heaney is often almost anonymous. As he tells us in 'Stations' (SP, 59), his first poems were published under the pseudonym 'Incertus' – as though he were as yet uncertain what his signature would be – and the youthful books contain a generic child as much as an individual one. This child is terrified of the rats in the barn and on the river-bank; he looks at his image in wells, and watches the cow in calf and the trout in the stream; he misses an old horse who has died; he gathers blackberries and is disturbed when they rot; he is fascinated by the water-diviner and the blacksmith, and by the servicing of the cow by the bull. To this extent, a broad and generalized pastoral directive governs the early self-portraits. Yet in several poems the idiosyncratic rises through the general, and these are, justly, the poems that have been much anthologized. They include 'Digging', 'Death of a Naturalist', 'Mid-Term Break', 'Personal Helicon', 'Relic of Memory', 'Anahorish', 'Oracle' and 'The Other Side'. Heaney included all of these in his *Selected Poems*. What makes them more individual than many others in his first three books?

In 'Oracle' it is the announcement of the poetic vocation: the generalized pastoral child would not have thought of himself in retrospect as 'the lobe and larynx / of the leafy places'. The sheer peculiarity of these two lines, in which a person is reduced, by synecdoche, to two biological parts – an earlobe and a voice-box – draws the portrait of the child in a way that the more generic poems do not. In 'Digging' the child who carried a bottle of milk to his turf-digging grandfather, and who picked potatoes spaded out of their drills by his father, has to believe, now that he has become a man, that his pen is a digging instrument too:

> I've no spade to follow men like them.

> Between my finger and my thumb
> The squat pen rests.
> I'll dig with it.

> [DN, 2]

The disturbing thing about 'Digging' is that the Irish

Catholic child grew up between the offers of two instruments: the spade and the gun. 'Choose,' said two opposing voices from his culture: 'Inherit the farm,' said agricultural tradition; 'Take up arms,' said Republican militarism. And indeed the poet's first thought had been to measure, so to speak, the pen against the sword: 'Between my finger and my thumb / The squat pen rests; snug as a gun' (DN, 1). This is to conceive of writing as, like war, politics by other means. It is significant that in this – the first poem in his first book – Heaney rejects the concept of writing as aggression, and chooses the spade as his final analogue for his pen: the pen will serve as an instrument of exploration and excavation, yielding warmth (like his grandfather's turf for fires) and nourishment (like his father's potatoes).

But it is not only in the child as future poet (as in 'Oracle', 'Digging' and 'Personal Helicon') that we find something non-generic about the boy of Heaney's childhood poems. Like Wordsworth's boy of Winander, this is a child who thinks more than the usual pastoral child does. It is the intellectual shock of the revision of his initial knowledge of sex that sets the child of 'Death of a Naturalist' – the title poem of Heaney's first book – aswarm with inchoate feelings of curiosity, terror and disgust. The innocent schoolteacher version of sex (phrased in the naive voice of the child retelling his school day) sets the scene:

> Miss Walls would tell us how
> The daddy frog was called a bullfrog
> And how he croaked and how the mammy frog
> Laid hundreds of little eggs and this was
> Frogspawn.

But then, with the advent of pre-adolescence, the real frogs come; and all the force of this child's unusual sensibility projects itself on the (blameless) frogs croaking their spring mating-songs in the festering flax-dam. In Heaney's most virtuosic moment of sound in *Death of a Naturalist*, the frogs' sexual noises awaken self-lacerating shame in the boy, as the smear of 'frogspawn' contaminates innocence:

> Right down the dam gross-bellied frogs were cocked
> On sods: their loose necks pulsed like sails. Some
>   hopped:
> The slap and plop were obscene threats. Some sat
> Poised like mud-grenades, their blunt heads farting.
> I sickened, turned, and ran. The great slime kings
> Were gathered there for vengeance and I knew
> That if I dipped my hand the spawn would clutch it.

> [DN, 3–4]

Thus 'dies' the dutiful child who used to like watching frogspawn turn into tadpoles, and who believed the teacher's sanitized version of the deepest propulsion of animate life. Heaney turned loose all his thickest and most resonant orchestration ('cocked', 'hopped', 'plop'; 'pulsed', 'blunt', 'clutch') for this adolescent cartoon-version of sexual desire: neither Wordsworth nor Keats nor Hopkins would have quite acknowledged that their stylistic inventions could be put to such a brutal use. Idyllic pastoral has been exploded by those mud-grenades, the frogs, and the consistency of finish in the more anonymous poems of rural piety has been grossly disturbed by the intrusion of introspective sexuality.

The most individualized of the first-person speakers in Heaney's childhood poems is the adolescent boy who narrates 'Mid-Term Break'; his four-year-old brother has been killed in an accident, and he has been called home from school for the wake and funeral. But though a neighbour ('big Jim Evans') is named, the speaker and the dead four-year-old are not. The wake of the child is in part described in ritualized post-Joycean terms:

    I was embarrassed
By old men standing up to shake my hand

And tell me they were 'sorry for my trouble',
Whispers informed strangers I was the eldest
Away at school. . . .

Next morning I went up into the room. Snowdrops
And candles soothed the bedside; I saw him
For the first time in six weeks. Paler now,

Wearing a poppy bruise on his left temple,
He lay in the four foot box as in his cot.

                    [DN, 15]

What is least Joycean and most Heaneyesque about the
poem is the portrait of the poet's mother – not idealized or
swooning in her sorrow in Joycean fashion, she is upright
and contained, even though overmastered by emotion: 'My
mother held my hand / In hers and coughed out angry
tearless sighs.' That brief passage is an index of how soon
Heaney broke free of Joycean unreality with respect to
women, and how well his own adjectival gift served him:
the conflict between 'angry' and 'sighs', and the violently
suppressed tears stifled under 'tearless' are all part of the
power of the line. The adolescent boy whose awareness
makes the mother's inscape unforgettable is the differentiated speaker who rises above stereotype and anonymity.
    If the anonymous nature of farm labour and the generic
perception of the anonymous rural child animate Heaney's
relatively idyllic first two books, his third book, *Wintering
Out* (1972), takes up anonymity with a different and new
sharpness, exposing the raw underside of rural 'decency',
and investigating the plight of women in a sexually

repressive culture. In 'Limbo' a newborn baby, never christ-
ened and therefore never given a name, is drowned by its
shamed mother and dragged up by fishermen; in 'Bye-Child'
a nameless half-grown illegitimate child, incapable of
speech, is recovered from the henhouse where his mother
had confined him since his birth. For such poems, which
silently reprove the pieties condemning sexuality outside
marriage, Heaney abandoned the broad and placid pentameter that had served him well for poems about churning and
thatching and dowsing, turning instead to lines that are
short, sharp, taciturn and, for all their pity, 'cold' and 'lunar':

> Now limbo will be
>
> A cold glitter of souls
> Through some far briny zone.
> Even Christ's palms, unhealed,
> Smart and cannot fish there.
>
> [WO, 70]

(According to a medieval Catholic doctrine, once powerful
but now discarded, the souls of unbaptized children could
not enter heaven but were thought to be consigned to a
place called Limbo – from the Latin *limbus*, 'border' – where
they were denied the beatific vision, just as their bodies were
denied burial in consecrated ground.) Heaney's identification with the suffering mother of the 'small one thrown
back / To the waters' appears in his description of her
freezing wrists as she held the baby underwater (an action
euphemized as 'Ducking him tenderly'):

> I'm sure
> As she stood in the shallows
> Ducking him tenderly

Till the frozen knobs of her wrists
Were dead as the gravel,
He was a minnow with hooks
Tearing her open.

And would it have been better to let the baby live – only,
perhaps, to be confined like the 'Bye-Child' of the neigh-
bouring poem, the 'little henhouse boy' whose photo, says
the poet, is 'still / Glimpsed like a rodent / On the floor of
my mind'? Fed on scraps morning and evening through a
trapdoor, the henhouse boy sheds 'unchristened tears', and
now, freed, transmits silently

> a remote mime
> Of something beyond patience,
> Your gaping wordless proof
> Of lunar distances
> Travelled beyond love.

[WO, 71–2]

The ghost of rhyme is present in these harsh narrow-lined
poems (as the last quoted stanza reveals), but often Heaney
is willing to allow several lines to go by with nothing but
the occasional alliteration to bind his stanzas together pho-
netically. By turning his gaze from the abundances and con-
firming rituals of family life to a dark and cruel underside
of the culture he was bred in, and by directing his gaze away
from artisanry and agriculture to illegitimacy and intimidated women, Heaney admitted – in a characteristic enquiry
into facets of his culture that were taken for granted – longstanding 'anonymities' that were other than benevolent.

But *Wintering Out* also found a different sort of anonymity that was to prove immeasurably productive for Heaney:
this was the archaeological anonymity of the buried bodies
known to the poet from a book by a Danish archaeologist.

P. V. Glob's *The Bog People* (published by Faber in 1969),
described bodies of murder victims from the Iron Age preserved in peat bogs in Denmark. The book had an immediate and riveting effect on Heaney: 'The unforgettable
photographs of these victims blended in my mind with
photographs of atrocities, past and present, in the long rites
of Irish political and religious struggles' (P, 57–8). This
provoked in him 'a vow to go on pilgrimage' to see the
body known as 'the Tollund Man', accompanied by a feeling
that 'unless I was deeply in earnest about what I was saying,
I was simply invoking dangers for myself' (P, 58):

> Some day I will go to Aarhus
> To see his peat-brown head,
> The mild pods of his eye-lids,
> His pointed skin cap.
>
> In the flat country nearby . . .
>
> I will stand a long time. . . .
>
> Out there in Jutland
> In the old man-killing parishes
> I will feel lost,
> Unhappy and at home.

> [WO, 47–8]

'The Tollund Man' makes perhaps too explicit the equation
of the medieval corpse and those of 'four young brothers'
murdered in the early 1920s by the auxiliary police force,
the B Specials. The brothers were dragged by a train, their
'tell-tale skin and teeth / Flecking the sleepers' (WO, 48).
Balked by the impossibility of writing of the 'sectarian murders' (as they are called in Ireland) of the late sixties and

early seventies in the journalistic terms in which they had already been described by reporters and rumour, Heaney turned to the bog bodies as images of slaughter rising to view after centuries of secrecy. Their anonymity gave him an imaginative scope he would have been unwilling to assume in a literal retelling of local assassinations. The bog bodies also persuaded him that ritual killing had been a feature of Northern tribal culture in a wide geographical swath: that immediate history alone did not begin to explain the recrudescence of violence in Northern Ireland.

Second Thoughts

The largely benevolent picture of anonymous rural pieties – from the churning of butter ('Churning Day') to the family rosary ('The Other Side') – in Heaney's first three books is rethought in *Station Island* (1984) where, in 'The First King-dom' (from the sequence 'Sweeney Redivivus'), the anonymities are re-explored, this time in a savage self-correction by which early idealizations are brought sharply down to earth:

> The royal roads were cow paths.
> The queen mother hunkered on a stool
> and played the harpstrings of milk
> into a wooden pail.
> With seasoned sticks the nobles
> lorded it over the hindquarters of cattle. . . .
>
> They were two-faced and accommodating.
> And seed, breed and generation still
> they are holding on, every bit
> as pious and exacting and demeaned.

[SI, 101]

The voice of Sweeney – liberated from social constraint by having been changed to a bird – allows remarks Heaney does not utter elsewhere. Of course the most acerbic of these observations concern himself rather than his family: he, after all, was the one who exalted an ordinary farmstead into a 'royal' kingdom, and cattle-dealer relatives into 'nobles'. The violence of the poet's reaction in the last stanza of 'The First Kingdom' is his revenge on his own previous enhancement of reality.

And a second revisionary poem, 'In the Beech' (SI, 100), looks back to another time when the youthful poet ensconced himself in a tree; but he is no longer purely sequestered in nature as the innocent 'lobe and larynx / of the mossy places'. Now the tree is a boundary between the farm ('the bullocks' covert') and the larger world ('the concrete road'), and the boy – entering adolescence – experiences two new sensations as he hides in the tree. The first is his aesthetic reaction to the decorativeness of ivy twining around the tree: it reminds him of the leafy decoration on Greek columns:

> The very ivy
> puzzled its milk-tooth frills and tapers
> over the grain: was it bark or masonry?

The second sensation arises because the tree has a new function as a place of sexual privacy 'where the school-leaver discovered peace / to touch himself'. The tree is also a lookout on a wider world: the boy sees (it is wartime, and British tanks and planes are based in Ulster) 'the pilot with his goggles back [come] in / so low I could see the cockpit rivets'. Summed up, it is 'My tree of knowledge', where war for the first time disturbed the rural scene, and where the intertwining strands of adolescent consciousness – perceptual, social, aesthetic, sexual – find a location to make each others' acquaintance. The nostalgic idyll of the pre-social, pre-sexual 'secret nest' is now distant, judged by the ampler second thoughts of a fuller world.

These more individualized reflections in 'The First Kingdom' and 'In the Beech' reveal the constraints exercised on lyric when the poet resolves to speak in a purely anonymous (and often nostalgic) voice as the perpetuator in language of an archaic culture soon to disappear. It was inevitable that a wider social world should intrude on Heaney's pastoral: but it should not be forgotten that his early pastoral was not always idyllic (the croaking frogs, the rats in the barn, the 'stink' in the house on churning day, the weariness of the pregnant young farm wife in 'Mother', the illegitimate children of *Wintering Out*) and that his early eloquence was not reserved for the beautiful alone. To that degree, even his anonymities bore witness to a sharp and idiosyncratic observer silently arranging their tableaux and friezes.

2

Archaeologies:
North

the procession drags its tail
out of the Gap of the North
as its head already enters
the megalithic doorway.
        'Funeral Rites' [N, 8]

To enter the megalithic doorway is to go underground,
working back into what seems a bottomless pre-history, to
a 'matter of Ireland' more archaeo-cultural than agricultural,
and Heaney was brought to his archaeologies in *North*
(1975), as we shall see, by the violence unleashed in Ireland
from 1972 on. Earlier, in 1969, Heaney had closed his
second book, *Door into the Dark*, with a prophetic
poem called 'Bogland', in which the unearthing of buried
things from peat bogs was represented as instructive and
benevolent:

They've taken the skeleton
Of the Great Irish Elk
Out of the peat, set it up
An astounding crate full of air.

Butter sunk under
More than a hundred years
Was recovered salty and white.
The ground itself is kind, black butter

Melting and opening underfoot.

[DD, 55]

And though 'The wet centre is bottomless', 'Bogland' does
not envisage horrors to be found within it. Resisting the
usual image of bog-discovery – medieval gold objects –
Heaney clearly seeks either domestic ordinariness (butter)
or evolutionary astonishment (the giant elk). A comparable
childhood poem in *Door into the Dark* (37) praises the 'oat-
meal coloured' piece of petrified wood (a 'Relic of Memory')
retrieved from 'the lough waters' and stored on a shelf at
school. Other forms of stone – lava, meteorite, coal, and
even diamond – are unfavourably compared with it: they
cannot 'incarcerate ghosts / of sap and season' as the wood
does. Loughs and bogs contain Irish natural and domestic
history, and in 'Bogland' the poet enters history willingly,
as a 'pioneer . . . striking / Inwards and downwards' (DD,
56).

All this changes when archaeology ceases to be interesting
and beneficent, and instead is interrogated for an explanation of violence. Now, what Heaney's poetry (inspired by
P. V. Glob's *The Bog People*) retrieves from the bog is a
series of murdered bodies, serving as emblems of cultural
predisposition to tribal sacrifice. In 1972, when Heaney
published *Wintering Out*, Northern Irish violence had
already escalated: in 1969 British troops had been sent in
to Belfast and Derry; in 1971 internment without jury trial
had begun in Ulster, with over 1,500 people interned in the
first year; on 30 January 1972, 'Bloody Sunday', British

paratroopers fired upon Derry civil rights marchers, killing thirteen; and 'sectarian' violence (one of the many adjectives essayed to describe the events) reached new heights. But it was in the years between 1972 and 1975, when *North* was published, that Heaney's poetry was able to reflect more deeply on these events. 'The Troubles', like all complex historical events, have produced rival explanations: they have been seen as the aftermath of colonization; as the clash of religions; as class warfare; as ethnic disputes; or, in their degenerate forms, as the thuggery of rival gangs. No one living in Northern Ireland went unscathed by them; eventually everyone on both sides knew a friend or family member whose life had been changed (or ended) by them. In August of 1972 Heaney and his family left Belfast and moved to the Republic of Ireland, where they lived for four years in Glanmore, County Wicklow, in a gate-keeper's cottage attached to the Synge estate and rented to them by its owner, their friend Ann Saddlemeyer, editor of Synge's letters. Heaney resigned his lectureship at Queen's University and committed himself fully to writing poetry (free-lancing as a journalist and radio commentator to support his family).

Heaney had known as soon as he wrote *Wintering Out* (published just after the move to Glanmore) that a journalistic approach to the Troubles was bound to lead to cliché. His first attempt at dealing with current events – twelve lines that later, with one slight change, were used to close 'Whatever You Say, Say Nothing' in *North* – begins in realism: 'This morning from a dewy motorway / I saw the new camp for the internees.' However, the poem quickly subverts itself ('and it was déjà-vu, some film made / of Stalag 17'), and as quickly derides its own wish to insert the Troubles into some repetitive frame: 'We hug our little destiny again' (WO, 5). The usual journalistic and *bienpensant* remarks about the Troubles are later mercilessly exposed in 'Whatever You Say', and the poet does not spare

himself. The 'media-men and stringers' revel in their new
vocabulary; they have

> proved upon their pulses 'escalate',
> 'Backlash' and 'crack down', 'the provisional wing',
> 'Polarization' and 'long-standing hate'.

'Yet I live here, I live here too, I sing,' begins the poet, but
goes on to condemn himself,

> Expertly civil tongued with civil neighbours
> On the high wires of first wireless reports,
> Sucking the fake taste, the stony flavours
> Of those sanctioned, old, elaborate retorts:
>
> 'Oh, it's disgraceful, surely, I agree,'
> 'Where's it going to end?' 'It's getting worse.'
> 'They're murderers.' 'Internment, understandably . . .'
> The 'voice of sanity' is getting hoarse.

> [N, 51–2]

There is simply no room left in style for either reportage
or conventional ideology: 'The liberal papist note sounds
hollow.' Yet Heaney continues to believe that with a true
art, 'any of us / Could draw the line through bigotry and
sham / Given the right line, *aere perennius*' (N, 53). And so
Glob's book on the bog people strikes with electric effect
the poet seeking 'befitting emblems of adversity' (Yeats) or
'symbols adequate to our predicament' (Heaney, 'Feeling
into Words', P, 56). As Heaney said in a radio interview,

> My emotions, my feelings, whatever those instinc-
> tive energies are that have to be engaged for a
> poem, those energies quickened more when con-
> templating a victim, strangely, from 2,000 years ago

than they did from contemplating a man at the end
of a road being swept up into a plastic bag – I mean
the barman at the end of our road tried to carry
out a bomb and it blew up. Now there is of course
something terrible about that, but somehow language, words didn't live in the way I think they
have to live in a poem when they were hovering
over that kind of horror and pity.[4]

The poet recognizes adequate symbols by a 'first stirring of
the mind round a word or an image or a memory',[5] and must
then follow the symbol where it leads. The archaeology of
bodies is, for Heaney, such a symbol.

Having found the bog bodies, how is the poet to make
poems out of them? In 'The Tollund Man' Heaney
attempted a binocular view of the past and the present: on
the left, so to speak, the exhumed Iron Age body; on the
right the four murdered brothers and other 'stockinged
corpses / Laid out in the farmyards' after being ambushed.
The archaeological part is more imaginatively stirring than
the twentieth-century part, perhaps because the poet is put
on his mettle by having to delineate the improbable bog-
tanned body:

> . . . his peat-brown head,
> The mild pods of his eye-lids . . .
>
> His last gruel of winter seeds
> Caked in his stomach.
>
> [WO, 47]

But the power of the bog bodies has yet another component.
The archaeologists' conclusion that these are victims of
ritual sacrifice to an earth-goddess not only eroticizes the
naked corpse of the Tollund Man for the poet, but also

lends it the reliquary air of the preserved and exhibited
bodies of Catholic saints:

> Bridegroom to the goddess,
>
> She tightened her torc on him
> And opened her fen,
> Those dark juices working
> Him to a saint's kept body . . .
>
> Now his stained face
> Reposes at Aarhus.
>
> [WO, 47]

Expertly done though this is, and courageous as Heaney was
in allowing so much psychic material to be detonated by
Glob's book, the binocular poem is uneasy in proposing that
these sexual and religious interpretations have something to
do with the 'scattered . . . flesh', the 'tell-tale skin and teeth' of
the 1920s' corpses. The poem recovers itself in its conclusion,
where the speaker comes home to himself, imagining the
Tollund Man's last moments before execution:

> Something of his sad freedom
> As he rode the tumbril
> Should come to me, driving,
> Saying the names
>
> Tollund, Grauballe, Nebelgard . . .
>
> [WO, 48]

The 'sad freedom' of the certain knowledge of death – Hamlet's sad freedom in the last act – is bestowed on the young
poet (Heaney is still only thirty-three) by the apparent
repetitiveness of history. It happened at Tollund, it happened

at Grauballe, it is happening in Derry, it will happen elsewhere . . .

Because of the multiple and as yet intractable materials offered by the bog-bodies, Heaney 'rewrites' 'The Tollund Man' several times in *North*. The Tollund Man is twinned by the Grauballe Man (in Heaney's most beautiful 'bog poem', meditating on the relation between art and suffering); and there are twinned poems of female bodies – 'Bog Queen' and 'Punishment'. Understandably, the poems about the bog-bodies have been examined by literary historians chiefly as comments on the Troubles; and it is unlikely that Glob's book would have had the same effect on Heaney if Northern Ireland had been at peace. But if we recall that poems are the poet's attempt to replicate in words some version of himself, we can – without forgetting their function as symbols of a cultural predicament – come closer to their whole being as artworks.

Let me summarize briefly. 'The Grauballe Man' does not attempt the binocular vision of 'The Tollund Man', but withholds its contemporary application until the poet has completed his meditation on the bog-body. We are first given forty-five deeply imaginative lines for the preserved body of the Grauballe Man, almost vegetative, almost bronze:

> The grain of his wrists
> is like bog oak,
> the ball of his heel
>
> like a basalt egg. . . .
>
> Who will say 'corpse'
> to his vivid cast?
> Who will say 'body'
> to his opaque repose?

> [N, 28–9]

Then come the three shocking closing lines, throwing on the scale 'the actual weight / of each hooded victim, / slashed and dumped' (N, 29). It is affronting – after being lost in detached and even aesthetic contemplation of the archaeological specimen – to be subjected to the 'actual weight' of the 'slashed and dumped' contemporary. The poet overturns the objectivity of history by the insult of the actual, putting his contemplative power to aestheticize squarely in conflict with his political power to sympathize.

I have put this too crudely (because 'The Grauballe Man' has infinite nuance, revealing Heaney's gift for stunningly exact description better than any other poem in *North*), but the poem becomes a better artwork for having faced its own metaphysical stance so clearly. Is it wrong to aestheticize? Is it possible to do other than look objectively when what is before one's eyes is a long-dead corpse, and not a recently living person? What would the corpse himself say posthumously about his own state? Heaney answers this question in the regal poem 'Bog Queen', in which the corpse (this time an Irish one, and not a sacrificial victim) speaks out for herself, narrating, with delay and ceremony, her long stay in the bog. (She was discovered in 1781 by a turfcutter on the Moira estate south of Belfast and sold to Lady Moira.) For ten of her fourteen stanzas the bog queen rests undisturbed by human enquiry, and she is not resurrected until the last stanza: 'and I rose from the dark, / hacked bone'. In that final rising 'The Bog Queen' owes something to Plath's 'Lady Lazarus'; but before that, when she speaks, it is with the objectivity of one who can see her own disintegration. Gradually, she is 'digested' by natural process, and her adornments and garments decay. The narrative is eloquent and rich, as step by step the buried woman is undone until she becomes a geologic rather than a human phenomenon:

through my fabrics and skins
the seeps of winter
digested me,
the illiterate roots

pondered and died
in the cavings
of stomach and socket . . .

My diadem grew carious,
gemstones dropped
in the peat floe
like the bearings of history.

My sash was a black glacier
wrinkling, dyed weaves
and phoenician stitchwork
retted on my breasts'

soft moraines.

[N, 25-6]

What can be deduced about Heaney as a poet from such a sample? As the bog queen describes her slow changes, she has the equanimity of the dead, and she reaches almost the unintelligibility of a script in a lost language: as the two-thousand-year-long disintegration is narrated, her equal and far more surprising underground resistance to disintegration is not mentioned. After all – despite the 'creeping influences', the 'darkening' and 'fermenting' and 'reducing' and 'wrinkling' and 'soak[ing]' and 'fray[ing]' – the bog queen, once exhumed, is still unitary, recognizable, present. Heaney's even-handed attentions to brain and nails, pelvis and breasts, thighs and skull, hair and feet, 'realize' the body entire, with a blazon fuller than the convention normally allows. The bog queen is much changed, but (to use her own metaphor), she was only hibernating, and has now reappeared to testify to – to what?

First of all – if we recall Heaney's title and notice her regalia – to her nobility. Her (lost) diadem is the witness to that civilization of torcs and gemstones that Heaney had once rejected in favour of elk and butter as bog-treasure. She reveals not violence, like the other bog-bodies, but patience. Twice she says, 'I lay waiting.' When she rises, she rises not as a queen but as a woman 'robbed ... / barbered and stripped', her hair cut off, her skull hacked by the turfcutter's spade. She therefore gives off not her full radiance but 'frayed stitches, tufts, / small gleams on the bank'. Of course analogies can be drawn to the reduced state of the vision in this renovation of the aisling poem (a poem envisaging the nation as a maiden appearing to the poet); but the poem is also an assertion of the deep poetic interest Heaney now finds in the processes of unmaking, of the resonance he gives to the frayed, the hacked, the incomplete. For a poet like Heaney – who so loved the 'sloped honeycomb' of the ordered and butted and stapled thatch, who praised the 'heavy and rich, coagulated sunlight' that appeared on churning day, both when the butter was 'heaped up like gilded gravel in the bowl' and when it was civilized into 'soft printed slabs' in the pantry (DN, 9–10), who praised the retention of sap and seasons in the petrified stone – for such a poet to become the curator of undoing, of dilution, of loss, is to reverse direction with surprising force. Death having entered the poet's domain with such suddenness, he resolves to understand it, to live it out through the deliberate phases of the bog queen's undoing. Yet the process (thanks to the embalming power of the bog) stops short of entire disintegration; the poem asserts that something of the past is always preserved, and is always ready to be rediscovered. In spite of the bog queen's distress at her violation by the spade, she does not object to being exhumed: 'I lay waiting,' she has said twice, waiting for this very day. The bog body, then, in the person of this example who died naturally, can speak of the permanence of human nobility, not only of assassination and sacrifice. Heaney's respect for the complexity of the past, as one sort of bog-body balances another – the bog queen against the Tollund Man or Grauballe Man – is one factor in the greatness of *North*.

Heaney pursues his archaeology less successfully in the poem on the museum-display of the exhumed head of a girl ('Strange Fruit'), which relies too heavily on lavish but conventional adjectives: 'Murdered, forgotten, nameless, terrible / Beheaded girl' (N, 32). I have said that the bog poems are, for the poet, as much a replication of self as a symbolic representation of history, and this truth can be seen through 'Strange Fruit'. Here Heaney recognizes his own tendency to beatify and to venerate, and he finds this response inadequate to the girl's murder. Like an uninterpretable residue – or some other form of art beyond mimetic representation – the girl is seen 'outstaring axe / And beatification'. To the extent that the Tollund Man was 'a saint's kept body' reposing at Aarhus; to the extent that the bog queen is a resurrected goddess, so far has death been misrepresented, as Heaney's second thoughts advise him, and as his poem reproaches him. The bodies do not want to be beatified (religious language is inadequate to them), nor did they exist to be murdered (the language of violence is inadequate to them). What they claim now, and claimed in life, is what all human beings want: existence on the same terms as their fellows.

As Heaney wrote the bog poems, the archaeological and the contemporary converged more and more. It is the humanity, and the contemporaneity, of the bog corpse in 'Punishment' that has made this the most controversial of Heaney's archaeologies. Heaney makes the archaic murdered young woman ('the Windeby girl' disinterred in Northern Germany) one of his own ethnic group, a 'sister' to the Catholic women whose heads were shaved, and who themselves were tarred, for fraternizing in the seventies with British soldiers. Because he wants to correct his tendency to 'venerate' the bodies, to distance their suffering by aestheticizing them into museum objects, he confronts the 'little adulteress' directly. He first speaks about her in the third person and then, at the exact centre of the poem, speaks to her in a second-person address which he maintains to the end. 'I can feel,' the poet begins; 'I can see,' he continues: 'I almost love you,' he protests – but then he indicts himself: he was among those 'who stood dumb' while her 'betraying sisters . . . / cauled in tar, / wept by the railings'.

With 'Punishment', Heaney's archaeology of persons becomes an anthropology of the present: dig however deep, the person who rises to the surface is one you recognize from your own life. The situations of the past are replicated at the railings of Belfast. This cast of the imagination – in which the present (the tribal abuse of 'betraying' women) makes the past (the Windeby girl) suddenly relevant, and in which the past (the bog-body) makes the present (Heaney's own self-admitted complicity in the abuse) unignorable – is one for which Heaney has been condemned. But no poem is a poem unless, as Yeats said, it is about a quarrel within oneself: if Heaney had no ambivalence about the fraternizing women and their abusers, he would not have been moved to write the poem, saying,

[I] would connive
in civilized outrage
yet understand the exact
and tribal, intimate revenge.

[N, 31]

There are three criminal acts inventoried in the poem: the first is standing silent while 'punishment' is carried out; the second is 'conniving' in hypocritical condemnation of the act; and the third is the punishment itself, as the tribe takes its vengeance. The poet is not guilty of the third; but how many of his readers could honestly exempt themselves from the first and second crimes, those of which he accuses himself?

The best writing in 'Punishment' comes at the end. Though the language of archaeological discovery is, as it always is in Heaney, expert, as he describes the corpse – 'her shaved head / like a stubble of black corn, / her blindfold a soiled bandage' – the motive force within the poet is not the beauty of the blackened body (as in 'The Grauballe Man'), nor the back-and-forth comparison between historical past and journalistic present (as in 'The Tollund Man'), nor interest in the slow disintegration of the physical over time (as in 'Bog Queen'), but rather an examination of conscience with respect to personal behaviour. The line between past and present has reached its vanishing point: and whereas the poet did not stand personally guilty before the 'slashed and dumped' victims at the close of 'The Grauballe Man', he does stand self-indicted before the victims 'cauled in tar' at the close of 'Punishment'. The uses of the archaeology of bodies ends here, as past and present coincide. In the self-indictment of the end the poet has passed beyond 'veneration' and beyond 'atrocity': he has replicated himself in the very posture of the silent onlooker.

In an attempt to go below or beyond journalistic explanations of the Troubles, Heaney turned in *North* to an archaeological myth averring that a wide practice of prehistoric violence, encompassing both the Scandinavian countries and Ireland, accounted for the survival of savage tribal conflict, which fundamentally was neither colonial nor sectarian, neither economic nor class-caused, but rather deeply

cultural. This was a way of saying that other countries have
religious differences without religious wars; that other countries endure deep rifts between classes without resorting
to murder; that other countries are postcolonial without
continuing to avenge grievances dating from the sixteenth
century. Can it be, Heaney proposes, that what we are seeing
is not Catholics against Protestants, or rich against poor, or
loyalist against nationalist, but rather a generalized cultural
approval of violence, dating back many centuries?

In the summer of 1969, when the police and residents of
Derry were involved in what came to be known as the 'Battle
of Bogside', Heaney was in Madrid, as he tells us in 'Singing
School'. He goes to the Prado and sees the Goyas, which
he recalls, for the purpose of the poem, in a climactic order.
First, the instant political reprisal captured in 'Shootings of
the Third of May' –

> the thrown-up arms
> And spasm of the rebel, the helmeted
> And knapsacked military, the efficient
> Rake of the fusillade.

This is murder under the cover of military order, as the
Napoleonic troops execute 'traitors'. Northern Ireland
knows about this, but so do many other countries. Second,
Goya's lavish allegorical 'nightmares':

> Saturn
> Jewelled in the blood of his own children,
> Gigantic Chaos turning his brute hips
> Over the world.

Northern Ireland knows about this, too; but again, it is not
alone in that experience. Finally, a Goya that comes closest

to the origins of Irish violence, as Heaney now understands it:

> Also, that holmgang
> Where two berserks club each other to death
> For honour's sake, greaved in a bog, and sinking.

[N, 63–4]

This mindless clubbing, without justification by war or other cause, is simply violence for the sake of violence, though the armed berserkers (from Old Norse 'bear' plus 'shirt', the dress of the frenzied warriors) invoke a primitive ideal of 'honour' to defend their suicidal slaughter. It is this form of mutual slaughter that Heaney wishes to anatomize in the culture of Ireland.

To go back to a prehistoric time before the current journalistic clichés apply, Heaney returns, in 'Funeral Rites', to the Boyne valley and its megalithic tombs, built in a time when, it is presumed from archaeological evidence, human sacrifice was still practised in Ireland, and tribal war was endemic:

> Now as news comes in
> of each neighbourly murder
> we pine for ceremony,
> customary rhythms:
>
> the temperate footsteps
> of a cortège, winding past
> each blinded home.
> I would restore
>
> the great chambers of Boyne,
> prepare a sepulchre
> under the cupmarked stones. . . .

Quiet as a serpent
in its grassy boulevard
the procession drags its tail
out of the Gap of the North
as its head already enters
the megalithic doorway.

[N, 7-8]

This eerily liturgical piece of writing reveals a wholly male
procession from North to South, one so long that when its
head reaches the tombs north-west of Dublin, its serpentine
tail is still at 'the Gap of the North' at Carlingford Lough.
The 'somnambulant women' of the tribe have been left
behind to imagine the 'slow triumph' of the men – '*our* slow
triumph,' says the poet, speaking as one of the participants
in this 'neighbourly' ritual following on 'each neighbourly
murder'. Instead of intensifying anger or grief, the funeral
acts as a narcotic, on the men as well as the women: once
the tomb mouth has been closed again by its great stone,
the procession winds back north, 'the cud of memory /
allayed for once, arbitration / of the feud placated.' The
step-by-step advance of the lines; the religious ceremony
of the cortège; the unstated conflict between a Christ-like
'sepulchre' and an immense 'serpent' approaching it; the
attempt to dignify violent death by fiat ('I would restore /
the great chambers of Boyne / prepare a sepulchre / under
the cupmarked stones'); the savage understatement of 'each
neighbourly murder' – all these are part of the new civil
motions in which the poet, however unwillingly, finds himself a participant. Though he imagines a possible cessation
to conflict in the image of Gunnar Hamundarson, from
Njal's Saga, who, though dead by violence, was deliberately
left unavenged, Heaney's perennial hope remains unfulfilled
in the moment of the writing of the poem.

Other archaeological remains – the Viking ships, one of them unearthed by archaeologists in Dublin – offer Heaney an occasion to counsel himself against the voyeuristic attraction to 'violence and epiphany' always endangering what has come to be known (and increasingly exploited by contemporary poets) as 'the poetry of witness'. Like the bog queen, the Viking raiders now lie as 'hacked and glinting' corpses, their ships petrifying in the earth, 'their long swords rusting'. It is the 'swimming tongue' of the longship itself – that superbly made and functional archaic object – that adjures the poet to

> Lie down
> in the word-hoard. . . .
> Compose in darkness. . . .
> Keep your eye clear
> as the bleb of the icicle.

> [N, 11]

Another sort of instruction is sought from excavated bones used as 'trial-pieces' by Viking artists; but though they show how an incised line following its own buoyant migrations can unfold itself into life-giving 'foliage, / bestiaries, / interlacings', this heavenly glimpse cannot be sufficient to times so grim as the present. In a parodic self-image of his archaeological excavations, Heaney becomes 'Hamlet the Dane',

> pinioned by ghosts
> and affections,

> murders and pieties,
> coming to consciousness

by jumping in graves,
dithering, blathering.

[N, 14]

The exhuming of symbols, both human and monumental,
can no more affect reality, Heaney mordantly argues, than
Hamlet's theatrical bravado as he leaps into Ophelia's grave.
With this turning on his own processes, Heaney leaves
behind the recourse to archaeology that, while it lasted,
gave him ways to distil his anguish, guilt and feelings of
complicity before the 'weary twisted emotions that are
rolled like a ball of hooks and sinkers in the heart' (P, 30).
No one could be more conscious than their author that
these poems alone could not tell everything about political
events and the feelings they evoked in the years between
1968 and 1975. Yet there is no other body of work about
those years that so wholly evokes the desperation and devas-
tation felt in that period. *North* reconstitutes, in powerful
symbolic form and tense imaginative language, the impact
of those years on one person. That so many readers, both
in Ireland and abroad, have found *North* an unforgettable
book means that Heaney's archaeologies have consolidated
the personal into the communicable.

Second Thoughts

Tombs, caves, tribal pasts – all the appurtenances of
archaeology – are blood-tinged and corpse-haunted in
North: the archaeology of the northlands alone has come to
usurp the very meaning of the word 'archaeology'. In the last
poem of *Station Island*, however, an alternative archaeology
comes into view – not entirely consoling, but at least not
blood-besmirched; primitive and tribal, but solacing rather

than murderous. It is the archaeology of Lascaux, the cave in the Dordogne where Neanderthal paintings – among them, one of a deer drinking at a pool – were first discovered in 1940. The unknown artists – older than the builders of the Boyne megalithic chambers or the honour-berserk Scandinavian warriors – took advantage of relief-variations in the stone of the cave walls in inventing and disposing their stylized images of animals. At the close of 'On the Road' the poet (in the person of the bird-king Sweeney, and using the 'archaic' thin stanza of *North*) contemplates coming to rest at last in Lascaux, the birthplace of Western art:

> I would migrate
> through a high cave mouth
> into an oaten, sun-warmed cliff,
>
> on down the soft-nubbed,
> clay-floored passage,
> face-brush, wing-flap,
> to the deepest chamber.
>
> There a drinking deer
> is cut into rock,
> its haunch and neck
> rise with the contours,
>
> the incised outline
> curves to a strained
> expectant muzzle
> and a nostril flared
>
> at a dried-up source.
> For my book of changes
> I would meditate
> that stone-faced vigil

until the long dumbfounded
spirit broke cover
to raise a dust
in the font of exhaustion.

[SI, 120–21]

Archaeological investigation can reveal not only dead bodies (whether victims or, like the bog queen, merely disintegrating organic forms) but also a solacing art. There is no pool yet for the poet to drink from: as the bird-Sweeney, he can only 'raise a dust / in the font of exhaustion'. Yet he hopes that the spirit can eventually refresh itself, like the deer at the source: to that end, he will keep vigil.

3

Anthropologies:
Field Work

gleanings and leavings
in the combs
of a fieldworker's archive.
'The Backward Look' (WO, 29–30)

The title of Heaney's 1979 volume *Field Work* has of course
an agricultural implication. But it is also a phrase used in
anthropology: 'Where did you do your field work?' In that
sense it implies investigation into a culture not one's own,
or at least one removed in time. Readers had already met
the notion of fieldwork in Heaney's poetry: in 'The Backward Look' in *Wintering Out* the poet recalls obsolete Irish-
language kennings for the snipe: *little goat of the air, / of the
evening, / little goat of the frost.* As the snipe disappears in
the air over the dangerous landscapes of the North, its
obsolescent Irish names disappear into 'a fieldworker's
archive'. The poet's 'backward look' watches as, in present-
day Ireland, snipe meets sniper:

he corkscrews away
into the vaults

that we live off, his flight
through the sniper's eyrie,
over twilit earthworks
and wall-steads,

disappearing among
gleanings and leavings
in the combs
of a fieldworker's archive.

[WO, 29–30]

   The Heaneys – Seamus and Marie, and their two young
sons Michael and Christopher – have moved to the Republic, to Glanmore in County Wicklow south of Dublin.
(Their daughter Catherine will be born there, and some
years later, after settling in Dublin, the Heaneys will buy
the Glanmore cottage.) The poet has now changed countries
in a political sense, if not a geographical one, and comes
among the new scenes and people of the Republic as a
'fieldworker' in an alternate culture; he is also (after living
in Belfast for years) once again living among fields, in a
rural setting. The work he has before him is to register the
new ambience and the new feelings it brings with it, while
keeping a connection with his Northern past.
   In *Field Work* Heaney makes an almost complete break with
both anonymity and archaeology. He is no longer the anonymous child of a quasi-medieval rusticity, nor the spectator of
a renewed archaic violence, symbolized by bodies long nameless. Rather, his poetry becomes recognizably that of an individual man engaged in ordinary domestic and social relations,
who writes in an idiom largely shorn of both archaism and
portent, his poems visibly kept at a middle level of both genre
and style. He is a husband, a father, a person with friends and
relatives – and increasingly an elegist.

In *Field Work* alone, there are six elegies: for Heaney's cousin Colum McCartney (ambushed and shot in a sectarian killing); for his friend the social worker Sean Armstrong (shot by a 'pointblank teatime bullet' (FW, 19); for the composer Sean O'Riada and the poet Robert Lowell; for an acquaintance, Louis O'Neill, victim of a bomb explosion ('Casualty'); and for the young Irish Catholic poet Francis Ledwidge, killed in action fighting for England in the First World War. Work in the field, in this sense, arises from the obligation of survivors to celebrate those who have died: with each person, the poet has had a separate relation; in each poem, an individual must be characterized and valued. The Heaney style – earlier so apt in conveying the immemorial and the immobile – is now called on to sketch the living as they were before their annihilation, and to do justice to the moment of extinction.

The problem of elegy is always to revisit death while not forgetting life, and the structure of any given elegy suggests the relation the poet postulates between those two central terms. In 'The Strand at Lough Beg' [FW, 17–18] death and life uneasily alternate. The death-vignette of Heaney's murdered cousin is a lurid one:

> I turn because the sweeping of your feet
> Has stopped behind me, to find you on your knees
> With blood and roadside muck in your hair and eyes.

Yet a moment earlier in the poem, the cousin's family were still enjoying their bucolic peace as

> Big-voiced scullions, herders, feelers round
> Haycocks and hindquarters, talkers in byres,
> Slow arbitrators of the burial ground.

Structural oscillations of this sort between murder and peace organize the whole of the McCartney elegy. We see first the cousin's untroubled drive 'out beneath the stars', then behold (in an allusion) the first malign foretaste of what is to come as the cousin's car passes the place 'Where Sweeney fled before the . . . demon pack / Blazing out of the ground, snapping and squealing'. No sooner has the ambush happened than the poem follows it with a glimpse of the cousin's idyllic home landscape: 'The lowland clays and waters of Lough Beg, / Church Island's spire, its soft treeline of yew.' If this paradisal scene is spoiled by duck shooters, with their 'spent cartridges, / Acrid, brassy, genital, ejected', it is calmed again by cattle grazing with 'unbewildered gaze' in an early mist. Upon this scene breaks the horrifying vision of the kneeling victim, which the poet attempts to soothe by washing and laying out the corpse.

This elegy, with its fitful alternation between peace and violence, violence and peace, though it may wish to represent social and geographical calm as normative (the cattle-dealers, the cattle, the peace of Church Island) and to find murder (even in the analogous form of duck-shooting) an unnatural and vicious interposition, yet, by its form, makes murder the norm, which peace can only briefly assuage. Though we infer from the structural recurrence of violence that once murder has happened, no true peace can be restored, the poem stops short of saying so in words, and ends pacifically and assuagingly with the rites of decency. As we shall see, in the most savage of his second thoughts, Heaney will, in 'Station Island', make Colum McCartney attack this very poem for its attempt to sweeten death's ravages.

The way Heaney's elegiac voice economically sketches the living can be seen as Robert Lowell is called up (in 'Elegy') with a few brief nouns and adjectives:

> helmsman, netsman, *retiarius*.
> That hand. Warding and grooming
> and amphibious . . .

army ('to defend the rights of small nations', as Ledwidge
wrote, quoted in Heaney's note) – seeing these, we might ask
(adapting Yeats's words on Maud Gonne), 'Which of his
forms has shown his substance right?' No wonder Heaney's
four sketches can lead only to his balked summary couplet:

> In you, our dead enigma, all the strains
> Criss-cross in useless equilibrium.

[FW, 60]

This is a couplet that could not have occurred in Heaney's
earlier poems, whether those of anonymity or those of
archaeology. The complication of the human social person-
ality – that one and the same person can be a Catholic and
a British soldier, a poet and a fighter, a lover of the Irish
countryside and a war-victim in Ypres – is the enigma that
Heaney, the anthropologist of his society, must now
confront.

An Irishman living in Sausalito (Sean Armstrong), an
American living in Ireland (Robert Lowell), an Irish Catholic serving under the English flag (Francis Ledwidge), John
Field, the Irish composer 'Dead in Moscow' (as it says on his
tombstone, according to Heaney's note), a Catholic (Louis
O'Neill) dying from a Catholic-set bomb – these random
situations, brought together by obituary necessity, show that
Irishness is not a unitary thing. Not all the Irish are in
Ireland always, and not all those inhabiting Ireland were
born there or will die there. These facts are inconvenient
to the unitary view of both nationalist propaganda and
single-minded mythology, but they are the very stuff of
cultural interest for an ethnographer or anthropologist. The
contrariness within a presumably unitary culture is most
visible in 'Casualty', where Heaney takes up the case of a
Northern Catholic acquaintance who (against a curfew

and bar-closing promulgated by the Catholic side on the day of the funeral of the thirteen victims of 'Bloody Sunday') went out for his usual nightly drink to a distant bar and was blown up by a bomb set by his own people. That is an inconvenient fact; but it is part of the history of what happens, though propagandists are not eager to mention it.

In *Field Work* Heaney is an anthropologist not only of the dead, but also of the living. If elegies take up one half of the book, domestic life with his wife and social occasions with friends make up the other half: and though there have been earlier poems about his wife and their marriage, Heaney's first extended treatment of the couple (the smallest anthropological unit) is found in *Field Work*. There was one notable marriage-poem ('Summer Home') in *Wintering Out*, a chilling account of a quarrel finally mended: its central image – set out in Heaney's quick notation – was that of a foul odour in the house, finally discovered to be maggots under a mat:

> Was it wind off the dumps
> or something in heat
>
> dogging us, the summer gone sour,
> a fouled nest incubating somewhere?
>
> Whose fault, I wondered, inquisitor
> of the possessed air.
>
> To realize suddenly,
> whip off the mat
>
> that was larval, moving –
> and scald, scald, scald.

[WO, 59]

'High Summer' in *Field Work* brings back the maggots, this time harmlessly bought in paper bags (during a holiday in France) as bait to catch fish. The couple, though troubled by the teething baby's night-crying, are happy enough, and all seems normal. But like a time-bomb, a forgotten bag of maggots lies in wait:

> On the last day, when I was clearing up,
> on a warm ledge I found a bag of maggots
> and opened it. A black
> and throbbing swarm came riddling out
> like newsreel of a police force run amok,
> sunspotting flies in gauzy meaty flight,
> the barristers and black berets of light.

[FW, 45–6]

For all the appearance of normalcy, the poet from the North, even when away from home, feels that at any moment society can go mad, exploding into swarms of police, barristers and black berets 'in meaty flight'. This is the image that now tensely underlies all the poet's dreams of domesticity, one from which even the sequestered dyad of the married couple is not exempt.

In the best-known marriage-group in *Field Work*, the ten poems called 'Glanmore Sonnets' (which ring changes on both Shakespearean and Italian forms), Heaney writes a deliberately middle-voiced Wordsworthian sequence, poems which he hopes will 'continue, hold, dispel, appease'. He is amused by the excess of rusticity in which he finds himself:

> This evening the cuckoo and the corncrake
> (So much, too much) consorted at twilight.
> It was all crepuscular and iambic.

He even makes an explicit comparison between his and his
wife Marie's situation in Glanmore and William and
Dorothy Wordsworth's in Dove Cottage, only to be hastily
interrupted by a protesting word from his wife:

> I had said earlier, 'I won't relapse
> From this strange loneliness I've brought us to.
> Dorothy and William –' She interrupts:
> 'You're not going to compare us two . . . ?'

[FW, 35]

Heaney hopes, in this domestic retreat, to create a new
hard-edged form of pastoral – 'I will break through,' he
says, 'what I glazed over / With perfect mist and peaceful
absences' (FW, 38). As the sequence goes on, the atmosphere darkens: in VII Heaney imagines, when he hears
weather warnings on the radio, a fierce storm:

> Sirens of the tundra,
> Of eel-road, seal-road, keel-road, whale-road raise
> Their wind-compounded keen behind the baize
> And drive the trawlers to the lee of Wicklow.

[FW, 39]

In VIII there is thunderlight and rain 'lush with omen', as
the memory of a mongoloid child in southern France mixes
with surreal fears:

> I thought of dew on armour and carrion.
> What would I met, blood-boltered, on the road?
> How deep into the woodpile sat the toad?
> What welters through this dark hush on the crops?

[FW, 40]

And, in IX, the invasion of the domestic by external threat is complete, in a poem that deserves – for its combination of the domestic, the wild, the classical, the agricultural, the medieval, the vicious and the terrified – to be quoted in full. The *ars poetica* that will be sufficient to all sides of this reality – or that can exist within it – seems unattainable to the poet. Yet he embarks on his Shakespearean sonnet-portrait of wife and husband, redefining – with a gusto that quickly vanishes in self-doubt – the genre of the love-poem:

> Outside the kitchen window a black rat
> Sways on the briar like infected fruit:
> 'It looked me through, it stared me out, I'm not
> Imagining things. Go you out to it.'
> Did we come to the wilderness for this?
> We have our burnished bay tree at the gate,
> Classical, hung with the reek of silage
> From the next farm, tart-leafed as inwit.
> Blood on a pitch-fork, blood on chaff and hay,
> Rats speared in the sweat and dust of threshing –
> What is my apology for poetry?
> The empty briar is swishing
> When I come down, and beyond, your face
> Haunts like a new moon glimpsed through tangled
>   glass.

> [FW, 41]

The rat and his imagined retinue of horrors banished, the Glanmore sonnets close with a pastoral dream. No longer Wordsworth and Dorothy (or the real couple they are with small children), the poet and his wife have become 'Lorenzo and Jessica in a cold climate. / Diarmuid and Grainne waiting to be found.' The first, Shakespearean metaphor still lies within the positive dimension of pastoral, even if transmuted

from the warmth of Venice to the chill of Wicklow; the
second, Celtic one, however, comes within the aura of
tragedy. Both metaphors are literary, both almost mythical;
the anthropologist suddenly seems to want to leave his level
cottage ground. But the poet turns the sequence back to the
domestic, to the occasion when the marriage was sanctioned
– not by clerical ceremony but by personal vow, recalling

> Our first night years ago in that hotel
> When you came with your deliberate kiss
> To raise us towards the lovely and painful
> Covenants of flesh; our separateness;
> The respite in our dewy dreaming faces.
>
> [FW, 42]

Idyllic though this is, and means to be, it introduces its down-
to-earth anthropological note in mentioning the hotel. The
poet of *Field Work* will not pretend to be above such details.

Nor will he – in other marriage poems, such as 'The
Skunk' – spare comedy. Reminded by his wife's 'head-down,
tail-up hunt in a bottom drawer / For the black plunge-line
nightdress', of the skunk that used to visit him on California
evenings when he was writing love-letters to his wife in
Ireland, he embarks on a remarkable and blasphemous
description:

> Up, black, striped and damasked like the chasuble
> At a funeral mass, the skunk's tail
> Paraded the skunk.
>
> [FW, 48]

'Like the *chasuble* at a *funeral mass*? – is nothing sacred?' Or
so some readers might react. But to the anthropologist every
detail is a trading counter, useful in so far as it illuminates.

The deadpan observation – skunk's tail; damasked striped chasuble; wife's head-down, tail-up stance; black nightdress – mixes levels and usages with an outsider's indifference to the decorum that a culture imposes on its members. A good deal is freed up in Heaney by his capacity for detachment in *Field Work*, his investment in the domestic 'music of what happens' (FW, 56).

Yet the guilt and anxiety natural to Heaney's temperament – acutely exacerbated in the years between 1968 and 1972 – are always lying in wait to spoil his middle-voiced pastoral, not only when a rat brings viciousness into the scene, but even during a day which, it seems, will succeed in 'laying down a perfect memory'. As 'Oysters' opens, Heaney has driven with friends to the west coast, through the Burren scenery of 'flowers and limestone'; in a cottage they are eating oysters, which taste freshly of the sea; and at first all is well, as the poet reacts in pure sensuous delight. (Heaney's senses often transmit themselves in language with an ecstatic acuteness.) Yet the poem's five cinquains that ought to stand for perfection – five stanzas multiplied by five lines per stanza – are instead shaken by inner disquiet, as the tranquil stanzas one and three are contradicted by the guilty stanzas two (concerning sexuality) and four (concerning class privilege). It will remain for the fifth stanza to try to resolve this inner quarrel. The first stanza offers sheer relish, spanning the mundane and the seraphic:

> Our shells clacked on the plates.
> My tongue was a filling estuary,
> My palate hung with starlight:
> As I tasted the salty Pleiades
> Orion dipped his foot into the water.

But the second stanza counters the first, presenting the oysters as 'alive and violated' objects, 'ripped and shucked and scattered', torn from the 'philandering sigh' of ocean. The third stanza attempts to recapture the idyll, citing the friends' deliberate hope of a perfect day (mocked lightly by the comic rhyme of 'memory' and 'crockery'):

> We had driven to that coast
> Through flowers and limestone
> And there we were, toasting friendship,
> Laying down a perfect memory
> In the cool of thatch and crockery.

But guilt recurs, as, in the fourth stanza, the poet places himself in the company of the colonizing Romans, bringing oysters ('packed deep in hay and snow') over the Alps to Rome:

> I see damp panniers disgorge
> The frond-lipped, brine-stung
> Glut of privilege.

Two male sins – exploiting women and exploiting the colonized – have surged up in the poet's consciousness, preventing him from being content in the present with his friends. 'And I was angry,' he says, at being so haunted: and he resolves to throw in his lot with the senses, with poetry, with freedom, with aliveness itself:

> And was angry that my trust could not repose
> In the clear light, like poetry or freedom
> Leaning in from sea. I ate the day
> Deliberately, that its tang
> Might quicken me all into verb, pure verb.

[FW, 11]

This remarkable ending harks back to 'Peninsula' and forward to 'Postscript', both mentioned earlier. The belief in the senses as the indispensable base on which poetry (and freedom) must be founded animates all three poems; but where 'Peninsula' is about stored sense-memory, and is written from an anonymous solitude in Heaney's 'material' mode; and where 'Postscript' is about immediate sense-experience, and is written from the fragility and transience of the self in Heaney's 'metaphysical' mode; 'Oysters', defiantly positivistic and social, is about shared eating and friendship, and is written from the convinced will of the companioned self in Heaney's 'anthropological' mode.

Heaney's vow – to remain in the imperfect world of persons without letting social and human imperfection obviate all trust and friendship – gives *Field Work* its anti-Edenic stance. Heaney argues, in the four-poem title-sequence, that all perfection is maculate: the vaccination mark on his wife's thigh is one symbol of that marring trace on the otherwise perfect; and even the vaccination mark has to be added to, by the poet's 'priming' the skin of his wife's hand with a leaf pressed to it, and then 'anointing' with earth the part moistened by 'leaf-juice', till the shape of the leaf appears like a birthmark on the hand. This self-invented ritual ends with a hymn:

> my umber one,
> you are stained, stained
> to perfection.

> [FW, 55]

Concessions such as this to the perennial Heaney reverence are contradicted by the poems revealing the couple's life, both in the Glanmore cottage and earlier, as one composed of uneventful details: putting on a record in Glanmore, recalling the party the night before they first went to America, when

they lifted the roof for us in Belfast,
Hammond, Gunn and McAloon
in full cry till the dawn chorus,
insouciant and purposeful.

[FW, 43]

The proper names situate the Heaneys in social exchange,
where people are not being reverent or sublime or aghast,
but merely 'insouciant and purposeful'.

Or angry and reproachful, as in 'An Afterwards', when
the poet (already intensely reading Dante and translating
the passage on Ugolino) imagines himself in the ninth circle
of hell, as his widow comes from the upper life to indict
him and all poets, saying:

'I have closed my widowed ears
To the sulphurous news of poets and poetry.
Why could you not have, oftener, in our years

Unclenched, and come down laughing from your room
And walked the twilight with me and your children –
Like that one evening of elder bloom
And hay, when the wild roses were fading?'

And (as some maker gaffs me in the neck)
'You weren't the worst. You aspired to a kind,
Indifferent, faults-on-both-sides tact.
You left us first, and then those books, behind.'

[FW, 134]

This of course owes something to Lowell's quotations from
his wife's letters in *The Dolphin*; but one has only to reflect
on how impossible it is to find such colloquiality in Heaney's
first two books to see how – with the help of such poems

as 'Whatever You Say Say Nothing' in *North* – he has
levelled his voice to the conversational, turned his anthropological gaze to the ordinary ways life is lived, and become
able, as a fieldworker, to sketch psychological and cultural
transactions.

There are, naturally, aspects of *Field Work* that look backward or forward ('The Harvest Bow' looks back to Heaney's
father and his practice of a rural craft, while 'A Drink of
Water' resembles in its clear visuality some of the later
'squarings'). And there are poems of selfhood (notably 'The
Badgers') that I will reserve for the consideration of
Heaney's alter egos in the next chapter. But what one chiefly
takes away from *Field Work* is Heaney's deliberate choice
to remain on the human, colloquial, everyday level – to
remain there even for elegies, which normally tend towards
apotheosis, and even for love-poems, which normally tend
towards the elevatingly idealized.

Second Thoughts

I have said that Heaney decides to do un-sublime elegies,
to station his elegiac subjects at the level of daily life – in
a fishing boat (Louis O'Neill), in the grasses on Church
island (Colum McCartney), in a living-room (Sean Armstrong), at the keyboard (Sean O'Riada), at the Glanmore
gate (Robert Lowell). (The exception is Francis Ledwidge,
where the elegy, though it forgoes apotheosis, ends on a
glimpse of buried English soldiers, and does not return
Ledwidge to Slane or Drogheda.) There are conspicuously
no gods in these *Field Work* elegies, and one could read
them all as part of the distinctive (and often successful)
modernist effort to rewrite, in more believable terms, the
heroic, sublime and religious conventions of the classical
elegy.

Yet when it becomes time to elegize his own father (Patrick Heaney died in October 1968), Heaney will rethink his elegiac practice. In 'The Stone Verdict' (appearing in *The Haw Lantern* in 1987) Heaney uses the art of the personal vignette – brought to such expertise in *Field Work* eight years earlier – to identify his father as an individual, both in physical outline and in psychological character. But the poet also invokes the idea of 'the judgment place' and 'the ultimate court', lifting the poem to a metaphysical level that goes beyond the human anthropological plane:

When he stands in the judgment place
With his stick in his hand and the broad hat
Still on his head, maimed by self-doubt
And an old disdain of sweet talk and excuses,
It will be no justice if the sentence is blabbed out.
He will expect more than words in the ultimate court
He relied on through a lifetime's speechlessness.

Heaney must now imagine what sort of verdict his father – whose silent integrity was mistrustful of speech – would recognize and assent to. The poet is driven to myth (one he drew, as he has said in conversation, from W. K. C. Guthrie's *The Greeks and Their Gods*):

Hermes then is an ancient god of the countryside, named by the Greeks from the *herma*, also called *hermaion*, which was a cairn or heap of stones. These cairns served as landmarks . . . To explain the connexion of Hermes with the cairns, the Greeks characteristically invented an aetiological myth. When Hermes killed Argos, he was brought to trial by the gods. They acquitted him, and in doing so each threw his voting-pebble (*phethos*) at his feet. Thus a heap of stones grew up around him.[6]

This form of voting by solid things, Heaney thinks, would be the appropriate form of judgment-process for his father:

> Let it be like the judgment of Hermes,
> God of the stone heap, where the stones were verdicts
> Cast solidly at his feet, piling up around him
> Until he stood waist deep in the cairn
> Of his apotheosis . . .

But with the mythical analogy established, Heaney returns – in *Field Work* mode – to the ordinary, to local piles of stones that his father might well have stood among: 'maybe a gate-pillar / Or a tumbled wallstead where hogweed earths the silence. . . .' A *Field Work* poem might have ended there, with the son – after being temporarily constrained by love to seek an elegiac apotheosis through myth – descending to ground level. That 'The Stone Verdict' does not end in an 'earthed' closure is a sign of Heaney's new interest in the virtual realm, in which absence, not presence, defines a space. (This interest is the result of the deaths of both his parents, and is created by the poet's disbelief in personal immortality.) The silence surrounding Patrick Heaney's death is broken as one of the mourners, remarking on how places seem to be imbued for us with the spirits of those who have lived in them, is allowed to speak for the poet: the cairn of stones is

>   maybe a gate-pillar
> Or a tumbled wallstead where hogweed earths the
>   silence
> Somebody will break at last to say, 'Here
> His spirit lingers,' and will have said too much.

[HL, 17]

The last six words imply that Patrick Heaney would reject, in his reticence (as his son would reject, in his disbelief) such a wistful breath of nostalgic explicitness. Yet the son cannot forbear to attest to his own experience: that the world looks different when it contains an absence. It is in the last sonnet of 'Clearances', Heaney's elegiac sequence in memory of his mother (who had died in 1984), that the materiality of absence is most clearly asserted. But here, in 'The Stone Verdict', the would-be anthropological observer must make room for both the mythographer and the metaphysician of absence. The elegy for parents, whose death leaves a palpable gap in reality – or in what has been understood as reality since infancy – requires more than life-observation and humane memory. The rip in the very fabric of being itself must be enacted in the poem. The virtual realm of what is only imagined and cannot be observed will attain, after 1984, a pre-eminent place in Heaney's poetry. But between that moment and *Field Work* there lies the testing of vocation and belief represented by *Station Island*, a book in which Heaney confronts, in the form of revenants met at Lough Derg, all the other ways of life he might have chosen. It too is an anthropological book, but where *Field Work* remained among the living, *Station Island* performs an anthropology of the dead.

4

Alteritics and Alter Egos:
From Death of a Naturalist
to Station Island

How perilous is it to choose
not to love the life we're shown?
'The Badgers' (FW, 26)

Seamus Heaney's poetry returns repeatedly to questions of
identity and vocation: 'Who am I?' 'What life have I
chosen?' I have already mentioned some of Heaney's early
answers to these questions, both plural ('I am a descendant
of agricultural workers'; 'I am Irish') and singular ('I am a
husband'; 'I am a son'). In this chapter I want to treat
Heaney's self-definition through single persons *not* himself,
persons who serve as alterities (that is, opposites) or alter
egos (people he might have become). My chief text for this
purpose will be Heaney's long autobiographical poem-of-
alter-egos, 'Station Island', but I will begin with earlier, and
end with later, poems.

For a young poet like Heaney, born into a life-pattern
he knows he must leave, the first imperative psychological
task is to define his own selfhood. And a tempting (but
finally unrewarding) path to self-definition is to delineate
one's ethnic and aesthetic and ethical opposites. In Seamus
Heaney's case, this undertaking resulted in four relatively
early portraits of 'the other side' – one of Northern Ireland's
many euphemisms for the gulf between Catholics and

Protestants. Two of these poems – 'Docker' in *Death of a Naturalist* and 'Orange Drums, Tyrone, 1966' in *North* (neither included in the *Selected Poems*) – are hard, cartoon-like renditions 'from the outside' of Protestants. Both were written in the sixties, while Heaney was in his twenties; both show the unmistakable aggressiveness of a young man struggling for his own place in society, but also a curious flicker of sympathy, even for these culturally defined alterities.

In 'Docker' a Protestant shipyard worker (not, in fact, a docker; the dockers were generally Catholic, and the name was a mistake on Heaney's part) is defined in terms appropriated from his work. He is someone a Catholic would not want to meet at night on a dark street:

> There, in the corner, staring at his drink.
> The cap juts like a gantry's crossbeam,
> Cowling plated forehead and sledgehead jaw.
> Speech is clamped in the lips' vice.
>
> That fist would drop a hammer on a Catholic –
> Oh yes, that kind of thing could start again.

> [DN, 28]

The aesthetic that defines the docker – one composed of jutting machinery, steel plating, sledgehammer and fist, clamp and vice – is as far as conceivable from the aesthetic of receptivity and yielding that Heaney espoused from the beginning of his work, and expressed in 1974 in 'Feeling into Words': 'The crucial action is pre-verbal, to be able to allow the first alertness or come-hither, sensed in a blurred or incomplete way, to dilate and approach as a thought or a theme or a phrase' (P, 49).

The second repudiatory poem sketching 'the other side'

('Orange Drums, Tyrone, 1966') concerns the July marching season in Ulster, which celebrates the Protestant victory
over James II at the battle of the Boyne in 1690. In Heaney's
1966 poem 'It is the drums preside, like giant tumours',
with their stentorian aesthetic (N, [1975] 68). Yet in each of
these two stereotyping poems Heaney cannot keep entirely
aloof from his Protestant opposites. In the first, he draws the
docker into another stereotype, this time a pre-Reformation
unifying one: 'He sits, strong and blunt as a Celtic cross';
and in the second, the marcher bearing the Unionist drum
is felt to be oppressed and wounded by it: 'He is raised up
by what he buckles under. / . . . The pigskin's scourged until
his knuckles bleed.' These moments of sympathy would not
appear in the usual propaganda poem; yet they are not
enough to enable Heaney to identify entirely with the
worker or the drummer. The poems, because they originate
in stereotype, are unsatisfying, in spite of their brilliant
phrases.

A far more confident vignette, treating the uneasiness of
even cordial relations between the two 'sides', is offered
among Heaney's poems-in-prose that make up the sequence
'Stations' (1975). In 'Trial Runs' we find ourselves at the
close of the Second World War; a Protestant neighbour,
now demobilized, drops by (but does not enter) the
Heaneys' house with a present for the poet's father:

> In a khaki shirt and brass-buckled belt, a de-
> mobbed neighbour leaned against our jamb. My
> father jingled silver deep in both pockets and
> laughed when the big clicking rosary beads were
> produced.
> 'Did they make a papish of you over there?'
> 'Oh, damn the fear! I stole them for you, Paddy,
> off the pope's dresser when his back was turned.'
> 'You could harness a donkey with them.'

Their laughter sailed above my head, a hoarse
clamour, two big nervous birds dipping and lifting,
making trial runs over a territory.

[SP, 45]

In this Joycean epiphany the stereotypes are still present –
the half-military British dress of the neighbour, the hands-
in-pockets stance of the farmer, the worn sectarian joking
exchanged between them – but something else 'dips and
lifts' in the passage – the fact that the Protestant neighbour
has thought of Patrick Heaney when he was away at war,
that he has brought back as a gift not something he himself
would like, but something he thought the recipient would
like – a rosary, and a generously big one. The two men will
not be able to go farther into amiability than their awkward
joking; but the son hails it none the less as the marking out
of an intermediate territory where Catholic and Protestant
might feel neighbourly good will for each other rather than
enmity.

Comparable 'territory' of rapprochement is canvassed in
'The Other Side', a 1972 three-part sequence in which each
poem clusters round a remark made by the Heaneys' white-
haired and 'patriarchal' Protestant neighbour. In the first
part he criticizes the Heaneys' land: 'It's poor as Lazarus,
that ground.' In the second, he criticizes their religion:
'Your side of the house, I believe, / hardly rule by the book
at all.' But in the third, he cannot help himself from being
drawn into the Heaney hearthside: at evening he courteously (and embarrassedly) lingers outside the house till
they have finished the family prayers, and then knocks:

'A right-looking night,'
he might say, 'I was dandering by
and says I, I might as well call.'

Under such different (and confusing) aspects, the young
poet-to-be perceives the local incarnation of 'the other side'.
The neighbour appears sometimes, as in part I, a forbidding
superior, with 'his fabulous, biblical dismissal' of the Heaney
acres; sometimes, as in part II, a figure of mockery among
the Heaneys ('For days we would rehearse / each patriarchal
dictum'); and sometimes, as in part III, merely a fellow-
creature feeling estranged in the murmur of the unfamiliar
rosary he hears being recited behind the Heaney door. In
the evening vignette, which we see as on a stage divided in
two by the cottage door, the Heaneys pray inside the lighted
room at the left while the neighbour lingers in the dark at
the right. The adult poet is now, at the close of the poem,
the silent presence monitoring his own response to this
allegorical tableau of the separation between one's own side
and 'the other side':

> But now I stand behind him
> in the dark yard, in the moan of prayers.
> He puts a hand in a pocket
>
> or taps a little tune with the blackthorn
> shyly, as if he were party to lovemaking or a stranger's
>   weeping.
>
> Should I slip away, I wonder,
> or go up and touch his shoulder
> and talk about the weather
>
> or the price of grass-seed?
>
>   [WO, 36]

The silent proximity in the dark, the wavering query, the
impulse to touch, are gestures that the younger poet would

not have been capable of in the poems of the docker or the drummer. To realize how strange Catholic prayers would sound to a Protestant ('the rosary was dragging / mournfully on in the kitchen'); to understand the embarrassment in the neighbour's pause in the dark of the yard; to regret the stringently circumscribed form that talk between the two 'sides' must take (weather, crops) – all of this arises from Heaney's enlarged adult capacity for empathy. The mere complexity of the neighbour – which requires the three quotations, the three-part poem, in order to be represented in the round – suggests a marked advance in representational fidelity over the more stereotypical portraits of docker and drummer. A faceted, many-sided portrait – of the sort Heaney would later undertake in representing his mother in 'Clearances' – is here granted to someone outside the poet's ethnic group. And the poet's final question is one that Protestants of good will, it is intimated, might equally be posing to themselves: Are even superficial and conventional interactions (such as talk about 'the weather / or the price of grass-seed') preferable to a frozen and excluding cultural silence? Since connection holds the climactic position in Heaney's poem, it is intimated that the poet would rather touch (albeit briefly) and converse (albeit in the most ritualized way), than 'slip away' without making contact.

Heaney's wish to draw Protestant alterity into the scope of his portraiture is visible in two further poems of *Wintering Out*. The first ('The Wool Trade') is constructed on alterity, contrasting the phrase 'the wool trade', as it resonates richly in the mouth of Heaney's English interlocutor, with Heaney's own resistant sense of Protestant oppression – even to bloodshed – of Catholics: 'I must talk of tweed, / A stiff cloth with flecks like blood.' This simple opposition allies the poem to 'Docker' and 'Orange Drums'; but tucked within these opening and closing brackets we find Heaney's

nostalgia for 'a language of waterwheels, / A lost syntax of
looms and spindles', bringing Protestant artisanry in the
wool trade into the orbit of all the lost skills of which the
poet is the elegist (WO, 37). The other, more accomplished
poem of 'the other side' ('Linen Town') contemplates Belfast in 1786, twelve years before the hanging of the Protestant rebel Henry Joy McCracken, leader of the United
Irishmen in the Ulster insurrection of 1798. The narration
zigzags back and forth between the pristine and untroubled
Belfast seen in a 1786 print of its High Street and the
divided Belfast where, twelve years later, 'they hanged young
McCracken'. As the poet, in imagination, enters the serene
atmosphere of the print, he foretells what will destroy it:

> This lownecked belle and tricorned fop
>
> Still flourish undisturbed
> By the swinging tongue of his body.

At the close of the poem, the poet wishes with all his heart
that in 1798 things had taken a different turn, that 'reasonable light' had prevailed over political savagery:

> It's twenty to four
> On one of the last afternoons
> Of reasonable light.
>
> Smell the tidal Lagan:
> Take a last turn
> In the tang of possibility.
>
> [WO, 38]

The discretion and reserve of its close place this poem
within the tradition of the 'pen and ink, water tint' of the
eighteenth-century print, paying homage to its 'reasonable'

formal poise. Only the 'swinging tongue' of McCracken's body leans in from the future to shadow the Enlightenment elegance of the scene. Yet the poem suggests that just as this 'civic print' was changed in one (disastrous) direction, so perhaps a reverse 'unfreezing' of the present murderous scene might be accomplished, and 'reasonable light' might once again be the light in which daily life is lived. After all, the 'tang of possibility' is always available.

As Heaney grows older he no longer sees moral usefulness in focusing on alterity as such (though he returns to the kindness of a Protestant neighbour in 'An Ulster Twilight' in *Station Island*). Rather, the murdered victims – as civil rights marches and police reactions decline into undercover terrorism on both sides – haunt him more profoundly than political opposition or sectarian culture. The victims become increasingly a collective set of spectres (see Heaney's 'second thoughts' in 'Damson' (1996), treated at the end of this chapter). Moral enquiry no longer seems pursuable through investigation of 'the other side': it is more profitable to look to one's own character and sympathies, and test those for adequacy and breadth. Consequently, it is persons who resemble himself in some way, alter egos who are leading lives he might have led, or encountering a fate he might have encountered, who now begin to serve Heaney better as figures of self-definition.

From the beginning Heaney had looked to sympathetic alter egos in order to explain to himself his own position and function. At first these alter egos, as we have seen, were usually agriculturally timeless ones, collective workers or single artisans: the seed-cutters, the thatcher, the blacksmith, the digger. But Heaney also sought out, in other poems, specifically historicized alter egos, such as the Croppies who, not forsaking their militant principles, became in death unconscious bearers of resurrective nourishment. Then, in *Wintering Out*, with increasing sociological awareness,

Heaney focuses, through the old servant 'boy', on the inferior social status of Catholics in the North:

> Old work-whore, slave-
> blood, who stepped fair-hills
> under each bidder's eye
>
> and kept your patience
> and your counsel, how
> you draw me into
> your trail.
>
> [WO, 17]

In the same volume Heaney, feeling the impotence of the poet in modern society, assumes the garb of 'the last mummer' ignored by a family watching television, 'the luminous screen in the corner' (WO, 18). Heaney appears to accept, in the marginalization of thatcher and blacksmith, servant 'boy' and mummer, the increasing social obsolescence of the poet's art and service. These alter egos – though useful to the young Heaney – represent a dead end, and do not propose any alternative modern role for the poet.

Heaney's alter ego in *North*, as we have seen, was that of the comparative archaeologist, digging back past the early modern period to prehistoric times in order to propose an explanation for contemporary violence. From this remote perspective Heaney gained (as he implied retrospectively in 1980 when speaking of John Synge) an imaginative purchase comparable to that which Synge had discovered in his Aran experience:

> He had found a power-point, he was grafted to a tree that had roots touching the rock bottom, he had put on the armour of authentic pre-Christian vision which was a salvation from the fallen world

of Unionism and Nationalism, Catholicism and
Protestantism, Anglo and Irish, Celtic and Saxon –
all those bedevilling abstractions and circum-
stances.[7]

Synge died before he had to invent a counter-myth to Aran;
but Heaney, after his move to the Republic, could not continue (as *Field Work* amply demonstrates) with *North*'s metaphor of self-as-archaeologist. As squarely as he has ever
faced any change, Heaney examined – in the poem
'Exposure' on the last page of *North* – his new position, one
which removed him from the Ulster Troubles not in time
(as his archaeological alter ego had done) but in space, con-
signing him to a still unspecified role as observer of the
North from the Republic.

In 'Exposure' Heaney once more recalls words of
Edmund Spenser's – From *A View of the Present State of
Ireland* (1596) – which he himself had quoted earlier in 'Bog
Oak' and in his prose piece 'Belfast' (both published in
1972). In Cork Spenser had seen starving wood-kernes (Irish
soldiers driven to the hills by the English army) come out
of hiding in search of food: 'Out of every corner of the
woods and glens they came creeping forth upon their hands,
for their legs could not carry them. They looked like anatomies of death, they spake like ghosts crying out of their
graves.'[8] In order to define himself adequately in 'Exposure',
Heaney borrows from several available models. From the
Irish past he takes the role of sequestered wood-kerne; from
the classical past the figure of the exiled Ovid writing his
Black Sea *Tristia*; and from the recent past the (Russian)
role of 'inner émigré'. At the same time he rejects two other
roles – that of internee (as a political activist) and that of
informer (as spy or double agent). Such a set of self-
delineating figures testifies strongly to Heaney's need, as he
leaves the North, for re-invented metaphors of his own

position. No one of these analogies is entirely comprehensive: and the naked questions and doubts of 'Exposure' – intensified by the 'drops and let-downs' of the feminine endings of so many of its lines – cannot be resolved. The poet fears that he has elected the wrong life-role, and in consequence will have missed (in the strong masculine rhyme of the end) 'the comet's pulsing rose':

> How did I end up like this?
> I often think of my friends'
> Beautiful prismatic counselling
> And the anvil brains of some who hate me
>
> As I sit weighing and weighing
> My responsible *tristia*.
> For what? For the ear? For the people?
> For what is said behind-backs?
> . . .
> I am neither internee nor informer;
> An inner émigré, grown long-haired
> And thoughtful; a wood-kerne
>
> Escaped from the massacre,
> Taking protective colouring
> From bole and bark, feeling
> Every wind that blows;
>
> Who, blowing up these sparks
> For their meagre heat, have missed
> The once-in-a-lifetime portent,
> The comet's pulsing rose.

[N, 72–3]

These lines, justly ranked among Heaney's most powerful, gain their strength from their multiple self-images, the rapid sorting of self against almost any available 'other' – the friends who offer so many different 'colours' of advice, the enemies who hammer with hatred, the gossips commenting maliciously, even the far-focused Keatsian comet.

Earlier Heaney had looked to myth for an alter ego – to the story of Hercules and Antaeus. The 1966 poem 'Antaeus', which, though printed in *North*, properly belongs in *Door into the Dark*, is sympathetic to Antaeus, who was refreshed in strength whenever he touched the earth. Only at the end of this youthful poem does Antaeus envisage a destroyer who might 'plan, lifting me off the earth, / My elevation, my fall' (N, 12). In a caustic example of Heaney's 'second thoughts', the poem 'Hercules and Antaeus' – written in the seventies after the renewed outbreak of political conflict – transforms the defeated Antaeus into 'a sleeping giant' who may (so popular legend has it) once more awaken and triumph. 'Pap for the dispossessed,' comments Heaney bitterly, thinking of the way the oppressed batten on myths of ultimate victory:

> Hercules lifts his arms
> in a remorseless V,
> his triumph unassailed
> by the powers he has shaken
>
> and lifts and banks Antaeus
> high as a profiled ridge,
> a sleeping giant,
> pap for the dispossessed.

[N, 53]

To adopt the defeated Antaeus as an alter ego – as Heaney

had done in 1966 – is to condemn oneself to a lifetime of nostalgia for a vanished heroic past, living in 'a dream of loss and origins'. In 1975, conceding the victory to Hercules, Heaney resolutely says goodbye to Antaeus:

> The cradling dark,
> the river-veins, the secret gullies
> of his strength,
> the hatching grounds
>
> of cave and souterrain,
> he has bequeathed it all
> to elegists. Balor will die
> and Byrthnoth and Sitting Bull.

> [N, 52–3]

By bidding farewell to the chthonic elegiac myth of Antaeus, by finding something to praise in the 'spur of light' in 'the challenger's intelligence', Heaney opened himself to the more authentic – if more dubious and shifting – figures animating 'Exposure' – figures of exile, of flight, of sequestration and, above all, of second thoughts, 'weighing and weighing', as he says, 'my responsible *tristia*'.

In *Field Work* Heaney had essayed yet another form of alter ego – one not human but animal. This resulted in one of his most successful poems in that book, the numinous presence-poem 'The Badgers'. The poet, addressing himself, imagines the invisible but sensed badger as a revenant compounded of the murdered and the murderer:

> When the badger glimmered away
> into another garden
> you stood, half-lit with whiskey,
> sensing you had disturbed
> some soft returning.

> The murdered dead,
> you thought.
> But could it not have been
> some violent shattered boy
> nosing out what got mislaid
> between the cradle and the explosion,
> evenings when windows stood open
> and the compost smoked down the backs?

[FW, 25]

'What got mislaid' was the violent boy's soul, stunted and distorted in the life that led him to become a terrorist blown up in his own explosion. That life had begun on a farm not unlike Heaney's own, in a cottage with a compost pile 'down the backs'. Neither the poet nor his alter ego, the 'violent shattered boy', chose to follow the rural life to which they had been bred: and the poet's comparison of himself with the young terrorist leads to the great question which, with its image of that animal alter ego, the badger, closes the poem on an insistent rhyme:

> How perilous is it to choose
> not to love the life we're shown?
> His sturdy dirty body
> and interloping grovel.
> The intelligence in his bone.
> The unquestionable houseboy's shoulders
> that could have been my own.

[FW, 26]

The liberation afforded by using an animal as an alter ego is one that recurs when Heaney reinvents himself as a bird, the King Sweeney of Middle Irish legend.

It is from Heaney's metaphors of flight and exile that this

bird-self of Sweeney – one of Heaney's most successful alter egos – will arise. Sweeney, the king who went mad at the battle of Moira (AD 637) and, cursed by St Ronan, was transformed into a bird, is the hero of the medieval Irish poem *Buile Suibhne* ('The Madness of Sweeney'), which Heaney had begun to translate just after moving to Wicklow. He eventually published the translation as *Sweeney Astray* in 1983 (between *Field Work* in 1979 and *Station Island* in 1984). The poem – a third-person prose narrative interspersed with poems in Sweeney's first-person voice – is, in Heaney's words of introduction, 'a primer of lyric genres – laments, dialogues, litanies, rhapsodies, curses' (SA, unpaged front matter), and for that reason alone, appealed to Heaney; but its truest value for him appeared in what the translation stimulated – a suite of twenty original poems called 'Sweeney Redivivus', printed in *Station Island*.

Many of these poems are only tenuously connected to actual events in the Middle Irish narrative, but the fiction affords Heaney a strikingly new and hard-edged voice. I will come to this winged, exiled and 'mad' symbolic alter ego – and to its terse and ironic poems – at the end of this chapter, but will look first at the many realist alter egos visible in Heaney's long autobiographical narrative, 'Station Island', in which he revisits, no longer as a believer, a famous site of pilgrimage since the Middle Ages, the island in Lough Derg in Donegal to which he had come as a pilgrim in his youth (and where hundreds of people yearly arrive to fast, pray and undertake penitential exercises). In the Dantesque fiction of the poem the ghosts of Heaney's past come crowding thick and fast around him in twelve episodes, which Heaney composes in forms varying from blank verse to his closing terza rima in homage to Dante.

There are many ways to approach 'Station Island' – a poem full of persons, incidents and reflections. It has not been read as a collection of lives the poet might have led,

but I have always seen its dramatis personae as a series of
alter egos – men whose lives the poet, under other circum-
stances, might have found himself living. Within Heaney's
family culture three choices of life might have seemed plaus-
ible ones for the eldest son: to inherit and maintain the
farm; to become a priest; or to become a schoolmaster.
Heaney begins by rejecting the first (see 'Digging') and (if
we assume the usual Catholic suggestions to talented stu-
dents) the second. He decides at first to train as a teacher.
Yet the lives chosen by – or forced on – other men and
writers of (especially Northern) Ireland remain as parallel
existences in the poet's consciousness. Like the glossy young
priest of IV or the monk of XI, Heaney could have found
himself in religious life – at the missions or in Europe.
Like Simon Sweeney (the tinker of childhood memory who
erupts into section I), the poet is a 'Sabbath-breaker', but
he turns away from Catholic observance out of intellectual
conviction rather than outlawry. Though, like the nine-
teenth-century writer William Carleton of II, he leaves
Catholicism, unlike Carleton he does not become a Protestant. Like the chemist William Strathearn (remembered
by the poet as a member of his football team), killed by
gunmen pretending to seek medicine for a sick child (VII),
Heaney could have been caught in a sectarian ambush; like
his archaeologist friend who died at thirty-two of heart di-
sease (VIII), he might, given bad luck, have died early; like
his cousin Colum McCartney (VIII), Heaney could have
been the victim of an arbitrary sectarian killing. Like the
hit-man and hunger-striker of IX (based on Francis Hughes
of Bellaghy, whose family had known the Heaneys), the
poet could have – had he been brought up differently –
joined the many young men of his neighbourhood who
became members of the IRA. Finally, he both does and does
not choose 'exile': like Joyce (XII), he leaves his birthplace,
but unlike Joyce, he remains in Ireland.

I should add that although female presences in Heaney's
life appear in two sections of 'Station Island' (his Aunt Agnes
who died young in III, and the young girl with whom the
poet 'played houses' in VI), these figures do not speak, do
not become interlocutors of the poet as do the male figures
in the poem. The female presences were – according to the
poet in conversation – later additions to what first presented
itself as an all-male poem. In the Ireland of Heaney's youth
a young man's eyes were trained, in the search for his future,
on male models; and in spite of the two interpolations of
the feminine (and their respective symbolizing of the dolor-
ous and the erotic), the poem both implicitly and explicitly
asks, again and again, the question of male vocation. 'If you
did not follow my path' (the young priest might ask), 'why
not?' 'If you are like me' (a writer such as Joyce might say),
'why are you still in Ireland?' 'If you write poetry' (a victim
might cry), 'what good is it to me?'

In the comprehensive range of characterization and narration in 'Station Island' Heaney's dramatic powers (reflecting the moral choices offered him) display a steady
strength. Carleton's bite and anger and self-contempt –

> hard-mouthed Ribbonmen and Orange bigots
> made me into the old fork-tongued turncoat
> who mucked the byre of their politics –

[SI, 65]

are made to seem normal in the aura of corpses and bigotry.
And while there might seem to be balm in the obsequious
social approval offered a new priest – ' "Father" pronounced
with a fawning relish, / the sunlit tears of parents being
blessed' (SI, 69) – the poem, in the mutually critical colloquy
between priest and poet, harrowingly turns to the priest's
own horror at life in the foreign missions:

'The rain forest,' he said,
'you've never seen the like of it. I lasted

only a couple of years. Bare-breasted
women and rat-ribbed men. Everything wasted.
I rotted like a pear. I sweated masses . . .'

[SI, 69]

If the priest is repelled by his posting in the tropics, the poet
is repelled by the earlier parish welcome to the seminarian:

a clerical student home for the summer
doomed to the decent thing. Visiting neighbours.
Drinking tea and praising home-made bread.

Something in them would be ratified
when they saw you at the door in your black suit,
arriving like some sort of holy mascot.

[SI, 70]

The young priest, in return, making the implicit comparison
between the vocations of priest and poet (both of them
seeking some viable sanction for life), retorts accusingly:

'And you,' he faltered, 'what are you doing here
but the same thing? What possessed you?
I at least was young and unaware

that what I thought was chosen was convention.
But all this you were clear of you walked into
over again. And the god has, as they say, withdrawn.'

[SI, 70]

After repeated explicit and implicit testings of the poet's

own choices and fortunes compared with that of predecessors, mentors, friends and acquaintances, the question of
the purpose of Heaney's luck – still to be alive, still to be
able to exercise the vocation of poetry – is posed in its most
hostile form by the poet's ambushed cousin, who reproves
him for the way the poet reacted to his murder, both in life
and in the elegiac compunction of 'The Strand at Lough
Beg' (*Field Work*):

> 'You were there with poets when you got the word
> and stayed there with them, while your own flesh and
>   blood
> was carted to Bellaghy from the Fews.
> They showed more agitation at the news
> than you did. . . .
>
> You confused evasion and artistic tact.
> The Protestant who shot me through the head
> I accuse directly, but indirectly, you . . .
> for the way you whitewashed ugliness and drew
> the lovely blinds of the *Purgatorio*
> and saccharined my death with morning dew.'

[SI, 82 – 3]

This – though placed in the mouth of his cousin – is the
most vindictive and guilty of Heaney's 'second thoughts'
about his own writing, as it indicts the genre of elegy itself
– with its historical commitment to consolation and
apotheosis – if it 'whitewashes' the brute fact of murder and
'saccharines' the total annihilation of death.

All but one of the alter egos met by the poet in his
Dantesque encounters are from Northern Ireland. The
single exception to the rule is James Joyce – summoned up
in XII because neither of the Northern writers – Carleton

and Kavanagh – can give Heaney the advice he now needs
to hear, Joycean advice of 'silence, exile, and cunning'. In
IX the poet had burst out in an unnaturally explicit and
explosive passage of disgust, repudiating his identity and
origins, and despairing even of his power to revolt:

> 'I hate how quick I was to know my place.
> I hate where I was born, hate everything
> That made me biddable and unforthcoming.'
> . . .
> As if the cairnstone could defy the cairn.
> As if the eddy could reform the pool.

[SI, 85–6]

One might have expected that Heaney, as a poet, would
here have looked to Yeats as an example to hearten him.
But the cultural problems faced by the Anglo-Irish Yeats
do not closely resemble those encountered by Heaney, and
the poet turns instead to the writer whose experience more
nearly approximated his own. In the last vocational colloquy
of 'Station Island' Joyce, the most potent of these alter egos,
mordantly sets the poet free from his nationalist anxieties
and his familial inhibitions:

> The English language
> belongs to us. You are raking at dead fires,
>
> a waste of time for somebody your age.
> That subject people stuff is a cod's game,
> infantile, like your peasant pilgrimage.
>
> You lose more of yourself than you redeem
> doing the decent thing. Keep at a tangent.
> When they make the circle wide, it's time to swim

out on your own and fill the element
with signatures on your own frequency,
echo soundings, searches, probes, allurements,

elver-gleams in the dark of the whole sea.'

[SI, 93–4]

Though Joyce speaks in a language ('echo soundings ...
allurements, / elver-gleams') more Heaney's than his own,
Joyce's relation to his Irish subject matter – one of intimacy
paired with detachment, of affection modulated by scorn, of
absorbed tradition stimulating radical invention – offers more
to Heaney than the example of any other Irish alter ego.

'Station Island', in its testing of the poet's vocation against
that of other actual lived lives, brought Heaney firmly into
the domain of the demotic. The spellbound trance of iso-
lated child-contemplation, the oracular dark of the silent
Iron Age bodies, and the domestic sequestration of Glanmore have all been banished by the crowding and voluble
personages of Heaney's past. It is as though, by means of
the voices of victims and writers in 'Station Island', Heaney's
vocation has become clarified. He cannot neglect these present visitants who haunt his mind: he cannot retire into
fantasies of being a marginalized servant or mummer. He
must actively regard the present crisis, must let the contemporary victims 'speak for themselves' in ordinary colloquial
English through his (often abashed) mediation, yet must
retain an intellectual and moral independence – symbolized
by the work of Joyce – which resists the deflection and
deformation of art by either politics or pity.

The obligation to be faithful to historical circumstance
(of real lives, of real deaths) freights the poem with detail,
forbids it (except in the translation of John of the Cross
found in XI) the 'short swallow-flights of song' (Tennyson)

most congenial to the lyric. It must have come as a real
relief to Heaney, after the long sustained work of 'Station
Island', to compose the brief, alert and barbed poems of
'Sweeney Redivivus' – to take up a new alter ego, the vigilant
and tart Sweeney, whose bird's-eye view inspires lyric poems
as satiric and acerbic as any Heaney has ever written, while
also providing new forms of lyric solace.

From 'Sweeney Redivivus' I have already quoted 'The
First Kingdom', Heaney's second look at his family history,
and 'In the Beech', his second look at his tree-house, as well
as the poem that closes the sequence – the eloquent 'On
the Road', which finds its rest in contemplating the deer-
carving in the cave of Lascaux. In the Sweeney poems we
are allowed to see Heaney coming awake to a second life
in the Irish Republic, determined to go back again to re-scan
his past. In a Yeatsian image he unwinds the winding path
of that ball of twine, his consciousness, following its clue
until he is back in the cottage of his boyhood, listening to
his parents' 'sex-pruned and unfurtherable / moss-talk' –
talk which he will have to unlearn so as to devise his own
proper and poetic language. Heaney (as Sweeney) makes his
first flight away from those in his homeland who come to
stun him with stones, who pronounce him 'a feeder off
battlefields'; he recalls in another poem how the awakening
to sex ('the bark of the vixen in heat') 'broke the ice of
demure / and examplary stars', and liberated him imaginatively from his 'old clandestine / pre-Copernican night'. As
Christianity begins to thrive in archaic Ireland, paganism (in
the form of Sweeney) is marginalized, until Ronan finally, by
cursing Sweeney, changes him into a bird. But Sweeney
finds in the metamorphosis an unexpected profit:

> History that planted its standards
> on his gables and spires
> ousted me to the marches

of skulking and whingeing.
Or did I desert?
Give him his due, in the end

he opened my path to a kingdom
of such scope and neuter allegiance
my emptiness reigns at its whim.

[SI, 107–8]

What is 'neuter', however, at first feels 'empty' to
Sweeney the former king, used as he is to the heavy tethers
of place and role. The investigation of 'emptiness' and 'neutrality' will become of increasing importance to Heaney in
future books: for now, it is enough to notice the new language – *scope, neuter, emptiness, whim* – provoked by his
move south. From his eyrie Sweeney, in a fine flight of
medievalism, rails in 'The Scribes' against the narcissism
and backbiting of the writers of his kingdom:

I never warmed to them.
If they were excellent they were petulant
and jaggy as the holly tree
they rendered down for ink.
And if I never belonged among them,
They could never deny me my place.

Under the rumps of lettering
they herded myopic angers.
Resentment seeded in the uncurling
fernheads of their capitals.

It is unusual for Heaney to let loose such anger, even when
justified; he does it here more in defence of literature than
in defence of himself. He closes with this *défi* to the scribes
justifiably uttered by Sweeney (the composer of all the

beautiful lyrics of *Buile Suibhne*): 'Let them remember this not inconsiderable / contribution to their jealous art' (SI, 111).

The attraction of 'The Scribes' – besides its firmness, its satire and its irony – lies in its confident reproof of the scribes in their own linguistic and pictorial languages. One can hear the scrape of Anglo-Saxon in 'jaggy' and 'holly' and 'rumps' and 'herded' and 'angers'; one can see the hint of Irish pictorial convention in 'the uncurling / fernheads'; one senses the Latinity of 'lettering' and 'resentment' and 'capitals'. Sweeney's closing boast is deliberately made in scribal orotundity: they are not to ignore 'this not inconsiderable / contribution to their jealous art'. *Con-siderable* (*cum* plus *sidus*, 'constellation') implies the assemblage of elements into a constellated whole, as in *Buile Suibhne*; *con-tribution* (*cum* plus *tribuere*, 'to grant', from *tribus*, 'tribe') asserts, by summoning Sweeney's blood-link with the scribes, that they cannot repudiate him or his addition to their tribal literature; *jealous* (*zelosus*, from *zelos*, 'zeal') hints that what was once zeal in them has turned into its bad etymological descendant, jealousy. Heaney's etymological tuning-fork always rings true in such moments.

Just as, among the shorter poems of *Station Island*, Heaney's chosen example is the Chekhov who is able both to savour cognac and to 'shadow a convict guide through Sakhalin' (SI, 18–19), so the mentor-figure of 'Sweeney Redivivus' is Cézanne ('An Artist'), whose spare art – with its modernist resistance to both the luxurious chiaroscuro of Renaissance painting and the opulent *trompe-l'oeil* of conventional still-life – stands, in Heaney's eyes, as an ideal. Through Cézanne, Heaney warns himself away not only from aesthetic lapses into sentiment or excessive decorativeness but also from the moral lapse of attention to the opinion of others. Cézanne licenses the justified anger of the artist against whatever would corrupt art:

I love the thought of his anger.
His obstinacy against the rock, his coercion
of the substance from green apples . . .

the vulgarity of expecting ever
gratitude or admiration, which
would mean a stealing from him.

[SI, 116]

In spite of the bracing quality of the new ideals – scope,
neutrality, emptiness, whim, anger, obstinacy, coercion, for-
titude – which Heaney by means of 'Sweeney Redivivus'
calls to his own attention, the old ideals of his upbringing
hover with an obstinacy of their own, and refuse to be
jettisoned entirely. In the most clipped, dry and impeccable
of all the Sweeney poems, the poet contemplates a collection
of pictures he cannot bear to throw away, calling them by
the exalted name of 'The Old Icons'. There are three of
them. One is an etching of a patriot in jail, condemned
to be executed, his 'sentenced face' illuminated; one is an
oleograph of a clandestine outdoor mass in penal times, the
congregation soon to be undone by the arrival of British
soldiers; and the third is a drawing of a 1798 revolutionary committee soon to be betrayed by one of its members,
'neat-cuffs, third from left, at rear'. It is the informer whom
the poet finds 'more compelling than the rest of them':
he is the one who chose 'not to love the life [he was]
shown' ('The Badgers'), bringing himself to rack and others
to ruin. Though treachery, like murder, will out, its results,
diffused through history, remain for ever incalculable, 'inestimable':

The Old Icons

Why, when it was all over, did I hold on to them?

A patriot with folded arms in a shaft of light:
the barred cell window and his sentenced face
are the only bright spots in the little etching.

An oleograph of snowy hills, the outlawed priest's
red vestments, with the redcoats toiling closer
and the lookout coming like a fox across the gaps.

And the old committee of the sedition-mongers,
so well turned out in their clasped brogues and
    waistcoats,
the legend of their names an informer's list

prepared by neat-cuffs, third from left, at rear,
more compelling than the rest of them,
pivoting an action that was his rack

and others' ruin, the very rhythm of his name
a register of dear-bought treacheries
grown transparent now, and inestimable.

[SI, 117]

The means of 'The Old Icons' are concision, variation
and understatement. Each of the powerful 'old icons' is
described in a few lines; and each is a clear picture; yet the
namelessness of the figures depicted – emphasized by the
contrast with the 'names' on the 'informer's list' – suggests
that in the Northern Irish scene there has always been a
patriot; always a huddled Catholic minority; always a traitor.

The poet cannot throw the old icons away because they are
not outdated: everything has altered but nothing has changed.
Heaney here forsakes group anonymities not for archetypes,
as in the case of the bog people, but for avatars; yesterday
Robert Emmet, today Bobby Sands; yesterday the huddled
crowd at mass, today the huddled crowd at the civil rights
march; yesterday 'neat-cuffs' (according to Heaney, one
Leonard McNally of the United Irishmen), today – who?

Heaney's visual focus has never been sharper. In the
second stanza 'light', 'window' and 'bright' put a shaft of
illumination into each line, while in the third stanza, the
two antithetical spots of red – the priest's red vestments
and the redcoats – point up the ideological contrast as the
menacing present tense of visual art keeps the soldiers toiling closer and the lookout perpetually coming. The fourth
stanza begins in the same visual crispness, with the generic
clasped brogues and waistcoats, and with 'neat-cuffs' himself
geometrically situated in the grid of the group. But a second
movement in the poem – one that concerns itself with the
invisible – now begins to replace the visual one. This new
motif is at first unobtrusively inserted between the waistcoats and 'neat-cuffs, third from left, at rear'. The first invisible object we are privy to is the secret 'informer's list'.
The first invisible action we become aware of is neat-cuffs's
already-accomplished 'prepar[ing]' of that list, his 'dear-
bought treacheries'. The next invisible event hidden in the
icon is the future 'ruin' of the other members of the committee. And the next is the verdict of history, as the traitor's list
becomes 'legend', as 'the very rhythm of his name' becomes
synonymous with the register of betrayals.

All these 'invisibles' are of course now 'transparent'. That
is the usual outcome of the historical record. But how to
judge consequences? The very diffuseness of cause passing
into effect – the spreading ripple of catastrophe – vexes
judgement. The poem ends with the trope of ineffability,

the gesture which says, 'Words here fail.' And on the pivoting double 'now' – backward to 'transparent' and forward to 'inestimable' – the poem balances.

This passage from the visibilia of history to its invisibilia – from facts to consequences – is now what is most important to Heaney. Each of the old icons resonates with cultural consequence (though the moral is drawn only with respect to the third). Representation shades into aura, as fact subserves meditation. Heaney's poetry has never been more confident than in this instance, in which it hovers between the visual iconic (pictured but nameless), the historical (named and registered, but not iconic) and the 'auratic' – the felt, the legendary, the inestimable. All of these are important to the poet; and his poetry is most fulfilled when, as here, they find a way to coexist with presence and power. The alter ego of Sweeney gave Heaney the scope and freedom to write such eloquent and convincing poems. And, in their abstraction from the personal testimonies of 'Station Island', they form a bridge to Heaney's allegorical ventures in *The Haw Lantern*.

Second Thoughts

The continual carnage in Northern Ireland (visible in all the victims and terrorists of *Station Island*), together with his own removal to the Republic, compelled Heaney to gather representative alter egos – mythical, historical, contemporary, even animal – against whom and through whom to define his own being and function. As I said above, 'sides' become less important to Heaney than the sheer mounting body-count of his murdered fellows everywhere in the world, and the definitive image of that crowd of victims finally appears in mass-form in the poem 'Damson', published in *The Spirit Level* (1996).

'Damson' begins as the child-Heaney first sees a bleeding wound: he has been watching, with admiration, a bricklayer constructing a wall, with his sharp-edged trowel dipping and gleaming. Next to the bricklayer is his lunchbag, and the child notices a 'damson stain / That seeped through his packed lunch' from the bruised fruit inside. Suddenly, the man makes a false move and scrapes his knuckles; he holds his right hand, exuding blood, aloft, and the watching child takes from the blood a shock the poet's memory now resuscitates: the

> Wound that [he] saw
> In glutinous colour fifty years ago . . .
> Is weeping with the held-at-arm's length dead
> From everywhere and nowhere, here and now.

> [SL, 15]

At this memory, the thronging dead, always just at the edge of consciousness, emerge from their invisibility, summoned by the libation of the bricklayer's blood. They threaten to overwhelm the poet and his alter ego, the wounded 'trowel-wielder':

> Ghosts with their tongues out for a lick of blood
> Are crowding up the ladder, all unhealed,
> And some of them still rigged in bloody gear.

The insurgent bloody ghosts threaten to usurp the poet's imagination to the exclusion of everything else.

Heaney's understandable first reaction, remembering Odysseus (who with the libation of blood from the throat of a sacrificed lamb called shades from the dead), is to ask the bricklayer to help him to drive the ghosts back to Hades – that is, back to the conjectured blood-smeared place of

their murder, the lurid region of the poet's imagination
whence they came:

> Drive them back to the doorstep or the road
> Where they lay in their own blood once, in the hot
> Nausea and last gasp of dear life.
> Trowel-wielder, woundie, drive them off
> Like Odysseus in Hades lashing out
> With his sword that dug the trench and cut the throat
> Of the sacrificial lamb.

This is anyone's initial response to horrors rising up
in nightmare or recollection: a forcible repression. But
Heaney's second thought – which ends the poem by recalling the workman before he became emblematical of
blood, when he was merely a man wielding his trowel and
waiting to eat the damsons he had brought from home –
enables the poet to repatriate the ghosts not to the instant
of their murder (which is, after all, only the closing instant
of their history) but rather to the better, earlier and more
human days of their life at home. Do not follow the example
of Odysseus in your dealings with the ghosts, says the poet
(to himself as much as to the bricklayer):

> But not like him –
> Builder, not sacker, your shield the mortar board –
> Drive them back to the wine-dark taste of home,
> The smell of damsons simmering in a pot,
> Jam ladled thick and streaming down the sunlight.

[SL, 16]

In lieu of exorcism, or of maintaining the ghosts in their
status as victims, the poet chooses to reinstall the ghosts
into ordinariness – as his brothers, not haunters. The sunlit
kitchen scene of 'Damson' recalls Heaney's luminous mem-

ories in 'Sunlight' of his Aunt Mary Heaney baking bread
in the peaceful kitchen at Mossbawn. Heaney had set 'Sunlight' and 'The Seed Cutters' (with which I began this book)
as the dedicatory poems to *North* in order to counter the
blood-violence there: the two dedicatory poems show
people living ordinary lives in peaceful and coherent ways.
'The Seed Cutters' was a group portrait; but 'Sunlight' –
an incomparable poem of the idyllic within the straitened
– conveys a child's silent happiness inspired by adult love:

> There was a sunlit absence.
> The helmeted pump in the yard
> heated its iron,
> water honeyed
>
> in the slung bucket
> and the sun stood
> like a griddle cooling
> against the wall
>
> of each long afternoon.
> So, her hands scuffled
> over the bakeboard,
> the reddening stove
>
> sent its plaque of heat
> against her where she stood
> in a floury apron
> by the window.
>
> Now she dusts the board
> with a goose's wing,
> now sits, broad-lapped
> with whitened nails

and measling shins:
here is a space
again, the scone rising
to the tick of two clocks.

And here is love
like a tinsmith's scoop
sunk past its gleam
in the meal-bin.

[N, 8–9]

This exquisite genre-piece – in which the Vermeer-like glimpses of the anonymous woman who stands over her bakeboard at the window or sits waiting for the oven to heat are framed in front by 'a sunlit absence' and in back by 'a space again' while the scone rises in the empty kitchen – explains, in the last stanza, its deeply peaceful balance by the almost invisible gleam of love which is the source of the honeyed sunlit warmth of the poem. It is with a pang that one re-reads 'Sunlight' after the much later 'Damson', for now, into the Dutch light of idyll, there has come the streaming red of adult blood. The lurid red is transformed, it is true, into the 'wine-dark taste of home' by the alchemy of the damson jam-making: even red can be re-sanctified into the harmless activity of human beings absorbed in the dailiness of home. But that the red should ever have had to enter the sunlit sanctuary of the childhood kitchen, even if to be alchemized, is the scar the imagination cannot help but bear.

And although Heaney's surrogate 'trowel-wielder, woundie' harks back to the earlier artisanal alter egos of the poet's childhood, the artisanal scene itself has now become (in the opening lines of 'Damson') 'Gules and cement dust. A matte tacky blood / On the bricklayer's knuckles'. The new heraldry must contain not only the thatcher 'couchant' on his completed roof but also the bricklayer done in Keatsian 'gules' – another stylization of blood. It is by such means that Heaney's imagination re-thinks itself. His successive layering – in this case, of experience (jam-making) on earlier experience (breadmaking); of art ('Damson') on experience (bricklaying); and of art ('Damson') on art ('Sunlight') – makes each of his poems resonate with others that both precede and follow it. In adjuring his bricklayer alter ego against confining both the victims and himself in the atmosphere of blood and victimage, Heaney is warning himself against being seduced into the pornography of violence (a seduction too often visible in contemporary 'poetry of witness', especially that written by bystanders who are not themselves subject to the violence of which they write).

5

Allegories:
The Haw Lantern

a space
Utterly empty, utterly a source.
'Clearances', 8 (HL, 32)

Between the composition of *Station Island* (1984) and the
appearance of *The Haw Lantern* in 1987 Seamus Heaney's
parents, both in their seventies, died – Margaret Kathleen
(McCann) Heaney in 1984 and Patrick Heaney in 1986.
These deaths caused a tear in the fabric of Heaney's verse,
reflecting the way in which an inalterable emptiness had
replaced the reality that had been his since birth. The sonnet-
sequence 'Clearances', written in memory of his mother, ends
with an obituary: here the world is defined not by the presences moving within it, but by the etched absences of the
realia that used to be there. To open this obituary poem
Heaney borrows lines from 'Station Island' III, where he
recalled the early death of his Aunt Agnes. Her 'seaside trin-
ket, . . . a toy grotto', wrapped in tissue paper after her death
and laid aside in the 'big oak sideboard', was sometimes 'for-
aged after' by the poet as a fearful child. Whereas the little
grotto used to call up, to the child, the memory of its vanished owner, to the adult and agnostic poet of 'Station
Island' it summons the desolate and obscene image of the
decayed corpse of the family dog, discovered in a clearing:

I thought of walking round
and round a space utterly empty,
utterly a source, like the idea of sound;

like an absence stationed in the swamp-fed air
above a ring of walked-down grass and rushes
where we once found the bad carcass and scrags of hair
of our dog that had disappeared weeks before.

[SI, 68]

In view of the poet's disbelief in a Christian afterlife, in
view of the dissolution of the body, what can the poet say
in response to his mother's death? Heaney borrows, from
this death-passage in 'Station Island', two lines which now,
opening his mother's obituary, lead in a different direction:
not towards the mortal corpse but towards the son's memory
in which the mother lives on as 'a bright nowhere', 'a soul
ramifying' like a tree constantly putting forth new branches.
Heaney finds the analogy he has been seeking: when he was
born a chestnut tree was planted in the hedge before the
house; but his twin, the flower-decked tree, has long since
been cut down. None the less, the poet can 'see' it still:

I thought of walking round and round a space
Utterly empty, utterly a source
Where the decked chestnut tree had lost its place
In our front hedge above the wallflowers.
The white chips jumped and jumped and skited high.
I heard the hatchet's differentiated
Accurate cut, the crack, the sigh
And collapse of what luxuriated
Through the shocked tips and wreckage of it all.
Deep planted and long gone, my coeval
Chestnut from a jam jar in a hole,

Its heft and hush become a bright nowhere,
A soul ramifying and forever
Silent, beyond silence listened for.

[HL, 32]

The paradox of a living absence animates the sonnet. The sensual tactility of 'heft and hush', the irradiating force (after those softnesses) of the vivid vowel in 'bright', the infinite participial extension of 'ramifying', and the intense interior upward yearning in 'beyond silence listened for' are all 'alive'. But the livingness of all those moments has to be set against the sadness and concession in the fall of the feminine rhymes closing the last three lines, and the emptiness of 'nowhere . . . forever . . . silent . . . silence'. These difficult co-existences sum up the paradox that the poem exists to exemplify. The whole poem operates on this giving and taking away: as soon as we see the chestnut tree flower-decked, it has 'lost its place', yet against the burial baldness of 'hole' we find the 'utter source' of the ramifying 'soul'.

It is not too much to say, in fact, that *The Haw Lantern* is Heaney's first book of the virtual, a realm that the poet will continue to explore in *Seeing Things* and in *The Spirit Level*. The greatest re-orientation that can be demanded of a writer such as Heaney, so immediately responsive to the tactile and the palpable, is to direct his view towards the invisible, the virtual, to admit into representation those 'clearances' representing things that have been felled. In the seventh sonnet of 'Clearances', the one in which the poet's mother dies, her husband and children, standing by the bed, become acquainted with the death of that which bound them together. This is the passage – one of ultimate bareness of expression corresponding to the emptied space – that gives the elegiac sequence its title, 'Clearances' (a word with powerful historic reverberation in Ireland):

Then she was dead,
The searching for a pulsebeat was abandoned
And we all knew one thing by being there.
The space we stood around had been emptied
Into us to keep, it penetrated
Clearances that suddenly stood open.
High cries were felled and a pure change happened.

[HL, 31]

From the beginning Heaney's imagination had of course dealt in the invisible, but originally that crystalline realm of consciousness had been rooted in a sensual security almost equal to that of the real things that underpinned it. In the aftermath of churning and buttermaking, for instance, the material odour in the house is matched interiorly by immaterial after-images, after-sounds, after-smells, after-touches, imaging themselves in the mind:

The house would stink long after churning day . . .
And in the house we moved with gravid ease,
our brains turned crystals full of clean deal churns,
the plash and gurgle of the sour-breathed milk,
the pat and slap of small spades on wet lumps.

[DN, 10]

Before *The Haw Lantern*, a central aim of Heaney's art had been to turn the material world in this fashion into a crystalline one, even as the crystalline world became for him increasingly burdened by biographies, bodies and blood.

But the deaths of his parents – natural deaths, not deaths of violence – introduce a new strain into Heaney's art. An absence, one might say, becomes realer than presence. Heaney reverses himself: his aim is now to turn the crystalline, or virtual, absent realm into a material one – to make it visible by metaphors so ordinary as to be indubitable. The outline of the chestnut tree before it was felled is all the more ineradicable for being invisible; and once the mid-point in life has passed, one is as likely, in the surrounding landscape, to 'see' the vanished as the verifiable. *The Haw Lantern*'s insistence on the equality of presence between the material and the immaterial is brought to geometrical demonstration in the famous poem 'From the Frontier of Writing'. Its four opening tercets – in which the poet is stopped by a police road-block – are exactly matched by four appended and almost identical tercets, in which the poet is self-halted, while writing, at the frontier of conscience. We understand our invisible inner motions, Heaney implies, only by analogy with our experience in the material world. Like the obituary for Heaney's mother, 'From the Frontier of Writing' opens around a 'space' utterly empty and stilled, but this time the space is one of minatory 'nilness'. Its material hellishness and its spiritual purgation are emphasized by its rendition in a version of Dantesque terza rima:

From the Frontier of Writing

The tightness and the nilness round that space
when the car stops in the road, the troops inspect
its make and number, and, as one bends his face

towards your window, you catch sight of more
on a hill beyond, eyeing with intent
down cradled guns that hold you under cover

and everything is pure interrogation
until a rifle motions and you move
with guarded unconcerned acceleration,

> a little emptier, a little spent
> as always by that quiver in the self,
> subjugated, yet, and obedient.

This is what happens in material existence. And in the inner life? Though the only significant word that is exactly repeated in the second, 'invisible' half of the poem is *guns*, the inner scene of self-doubt is made to duplicate the scene outside: the frontier, the soldiers, the guns, the interrogation. When permission to pass is given, in the form of an inner liberation into writing, suddenly everything flows into a current, and the surface of things can once again be reflected in the 'polished windscreen' of inscription:

> So you drive on to the frontier of writing
> where it happens again. The guns on tripods;
> the sergeant with his on-off mike repeating
>
> data about you, waiting for the squawk
> of clearance; the marksman training down
> out of the sun upon you like a hawk.
>
> And suddenly you're through, arraigned yet freed,
> as if you'd passed from behind a waterfall
> on the black current of a tarmac road
>
> past armour-plated vehicles, out between
> the posted soldiers flowing and receding
> like tree shadows into the polished windscreen.

> [HL, 6]

The final freedom here is not yet that of Dante coming into upper air: the soldiers are still shadowing the mental windscreen, but they are gradually metamorphosing, almost, into the organic form of trees.

Did the (real) road-block turn up as a metaphor for a creative block, or did the subjugation of the writer at a real road-block make him aware of an inner equivalent when writing? In the poem the two possibilities balance each other, as material and immaterial tercets weigh equally on the scale-pans of the poem. What is certain is that for Heaney's Irish readers, road-blocks are a hated (and intensely remembered) fact of life, and to be made to pass through one twice in eight stanzas ensures a powerful visceral reaction, conferring solid reality on the invisible 'frontier of writing'.

Heaney writes many such parables in *The Haw Lantern*, and his debt to the allegorical and parabolic poetry (invented in part to defy Communist censorship) by Eastern European writers such as Vasko Popa, Czeslaw Milosz, Zbigniew Herbert and Miroslav Holub has been frequently mentioned. Yet Heaney's allegories are not written to escape the censor; they are written to escape the topicality of political journalism, on the one hand, and to define the realm of the invisible, on the other. The invisible, in Heaney's upbringing, was the prerogative of either nationalist politics or the Catholic religion. Heaney takes on, in *The Haw Lantern*, the job of exploring the use, to a secular mind, of metaphysical, ethical and spiritual categories of reference.

So in the wintry title poem of the volume the thorntree's red 'haw . . . burning out of season' is transmuted by the poet into an ethical object: the lantern carried by Diogenes as he seeks one just man. The small haw, in a trick of focus, is made to grow and diminish according to its function in the poem. At first it is its natural vegetative self, wanting no more than to be 'a small light for small people, / . . . not having to blind them with illumination', admonishing the poet against the grandiose, the oracular and the prophetic. This part of the poem takes up a modest five lines, an almost-sestet to introduce the more consequential octave that follows, in which the haw, as Diogenes' lantern, swells momentarily into mythical importance before resuming its 'eye-level' realistic smallness at the mention of the thorn-tree twig:

> But sometimes when your breath plumes in the frost
> it takes the roaming shape of Diogenes
> with his lantern, seeking one just man;
> so you end up scrutinized from behind the haw
> he holds up at eye-level on its twig.

The parabolic lantern rests so solidly on its material thorn-twig that (as with the road-block) one can hardly tell the actual from the metaphorical. In the last three lines the poem moves almost too fast for comprehension. The poet flinches before the haw's substantial integrity, its diagnostic needle-prick, its exemplary preservation of ripeness in spite of wounds, and its laser-scan of morality. Diogenes completes, in a swiftly passing moment, his scrutiny of you, his judgement of you. 'He holds up [the haw] at eye-level':

> and you flinch before its bonded pith and stone,
> its blood-prick that you wish would test and clear you,
> its pecked-at ripeness that scans you, then moves on.

By the end you have failed the test; the haw-lantern has moved on, and the one just man is still unfound.

The feature that makes the poem end so rapidly and confusingly – before one even has a chance to ask Diogenes to wait, to repeat his scan – is the non-alignment of its apparent parallelism. Each item is slightly out of kilter with its fellows:

You flinch before: a) its bonded pith and stone – a
                          quality inner to the haw;
                          b) its blood-prick – an action
                          potential to the haw, directed at
                          you;
                          c) its pecked-at ripeness – an
                          attribute (adjectival scarring from
                          peckings) outer to the haw,
                          bonded to the abstract
                          growth-point (ripeness) reached
                          by the inner haw;

You wish that:
Its blood-prick would   a) test you (first)
                          b) clear you (subsequently)
But
Its ripeness   a) scans you (transitive)
                          b) moves on (intransitive)

This is to schematize what takes place fluidly and incon-
spicuously: but Heaney's increasing deftness of syntactic
movement is one of the markers of his 'virtual' world, as
evident here as in the flowing and receding that close 'From
the Frontier of Writing'. In *The Haw Lantern*, whether
things are variously disappearing ('The Disappearing
Island'), 'assumed into fluorescence' ('The Milk Factory'),
travelling 'out of all knowing' ('In Memoriam: Robert Fitz-
gerald'), or written on the sand ('A Shooting Script'), they
are almost invisible, or soon to be.
    The inevitable filial depression in the wake of parental
death is most visible in the exquisite poem 'The Riddle',
which changes the Hades-myth of the daughters of Niobe,
who carried water in a sieve, into the poet's punishment –
to carry water in the never-ending riddle of value. If the
ethical category of justice is interrogated in 'The Haw

Lantern', it is the metaphysical category of value that is explored in 'The Riddle'. Here the poet describes the large mesh sieve used (before his time) for sifting, with something or other retained, something else falling through. Which was the valuable stuff – what was kept inside the sieve or what dropped down? Who can recall?

> You never saw it used but still can hear
> The sift and fall of stuff hopped on the mesh,
>
> Clods and buds in a little dust-up,
> The dribbled pile accruing under it.
>
> Which would be better, what sticks or what falls
>   through?
> Or does the choice itself create the value?

One can feel, reading this, the interior strain that Heaney experiences at the conjunction of his past inclination to the sensuous (*stuff, hopped, mesh, clods, buds, dust, dribbles*) and his present inclination to abstraction (*what would be better, choice, create, value*). It is a shock to come to the sixth line – like something out of an examination paper in philosophy – after the barn-dustiness of the first four lines, and after the colloquiality of the fifth. This shock of competing discourses gives the poem its momentum, and presses the reader to read on.

In ricochet, the poet pitches his imagination back to the sieve, but this time it is a virtual sieve, not a real one. He inscribes himself in a dumb-show, a mental 'mime' of sifting: 'Legs apart, deft-handed, start a mime / To sift the sense of things from what's imagined'. But is such a sifting possible? Is not the sense of things the starting point for 'what's imagined'? And does not what is imagined confer something on 'the sense of things'? It is a very Stevensian question, but Heaney will not give a Stevensian answer. Instead he reaches, in succession, for two phrases from his Catholic past. The first is 'culpable ignorance', the sin of one to whom the truth has been offered, but who determines to remain ignorant of it. It is the sin of those to whom the gospel has been preached but who provide only the stony ground on which the seed cannot take root. Heaney fears that he may, in his present disbelief, avoid the question of faith and value entirely. But then the poet remembers the second of his tag-phrases, the compelling notion of the *via negativa*. In 'negative theology' one can know God only by the 'negative way' of saying what He is not: He cannot die, He cannot suffer, He cannot change, He cannot do evil, and so on. In this definition of faith one adheres to piety by rejecting the false rather than by ascertaining the true. The 'drops and let-downs' provoked by death; the consequent erosion of one's sense of what life is or can be; the depression of uncertain 'sifting' – all these are elements of the metaphysical 'riddle':

> Legs apart, deft-handed, start a mime
> To sift the sense of things from what's imagined
>
> And work out what was happening in that story
> Of the man who carried water in a riddle.
>
> Was it culpable ignorance, or was it rather
> A *via negativa* through drops and let-downs?

[HL, 51]

Heaney enacts his 'drops and let-downs' not only through the falling line-ends – 'imagined', 'story', 'riddle', 'rather', 'let-downs' – but also by ending his riddle-poem in a question (it is the only poem in *The Haw Lantern* that ends this way). To employ the sieve-mesh and *via negativa* of poetic text (instead of 'taking a stand', as Heaney was often urged to do) is to seem to bring less water for a thirsting populace. A hortatory one-sided poem seems to solace human disquiet more than an equivocal set of riddling reflections which try to sort 'the sense of things from what's imagined'. Yet by being true to his drops and let-downs the poet may ultimately be of more use to his fellow-men than he would by rallying them too sanguinely to singly-conceived causes.

The Haw Lantern is an intellectual volume: it ponders; it values; it chooses; it judges. It examines the poet's tendency to 'second thoughts', which, like the *via negativa*, preclude a wholehearted embrace of any pre-formed ideology. Its great *apologia* is its poem of second thoughts, 'Terminus' – which paradoxically (and no doubt deliberately) has three parts. (Stevens: 'I was of three minds, / Like a tree / In which there are three blackbirds.') The border god Terminus looked both ways; so must the reflective poet. Heaney explains his compulsion to second thoughts by means of his upbringing on a farm in the industrial North, where he could as easily confront an iron bolt as an acorn, a factory as a mountain, a train as a horse, an Aesopian fable as a Christian proverb, a flowing stream as a containing streambank. The first two parts of the poem present its counter-pressures in resolutely left-right fashion, organizing them by the 'if' and 'when' of habitual action. But part III focuses not so much on those counter-pressures as on the boy who had to maintain his balance between them:

> Two buckets were easier carried than one.
> I grew up in between.
>
> My left hand placed the standard iron weight.
> My right tilted a last grain in the balance.

Baronies, parishes met where I was born.
When I stood on the central stepping stone

I was the last earl on horseback in midstream
Still parleying, in earshot of his peers.

[HL, 5]

No passage more strongly reveals the pull in Heaney
between the plain style and the elaborated style. The first
two couplets above are written in a style suitable to the
particular judgement, when one's soul is being weighed by
God. But as soon as the Norman vocabulary enters the
poem in the chime of 'baronies, parishes . . . parleying . . .
peers', something imagined, gilded and heraldic displaces
the parabolic yoke and scale-pans of plainness. From
Everyman to Earl; from gospel to romance – how could the
poet not have second thoughts when discourse itself offers
second thoughts with every etymology? The 'Flight of the
Earls' in 1607, as the last Gaelic chieftains (O'Neill and
O'Donnell) went into exile on the continent, ended the
possibility of co-existence between the indigenous Irish and
the English invaders. Characteristically, here as in 'Linen
Town', Heaney stops at the last moment of openness before
some irrevocable new step decisively changes the political
scene. To parley is to negotiate through speech (*parler*): it
is still the poet's function to stand at the border, in midstream, like Terminus, and try to keep speech alive between
contending parties.
Some of Heaney's metaphysical parables in *The Haw Lantern* are written in the plain language of a Bunyanesque
narrative; others range over a wide display of discourses.
Among these, the most autobiographical, 'From the Canton
of Expectation', sets a plaintive elder generation – resignedly
carrying out ritual nationalist practices of oratory, dance

and song – against a younger generation (Heaney's own) –
university-educated, activist, marching in the streets for civil
rights, demanding change. Yet Heaney does not permit his
own generation to carry the day. The poem is spoken by
one of the elders, fully conscious of the weariness of the
worn expectancies of nationalism, yet repelled by the hard-
headed phalanxes of the young. The spokesperson for the
old begins,

> We lived deep in a land of optative moods,
> under high, banked clouds of resignation.
> A rustle of loss in the phrase *Not in our lifetime*,
> the broken nerve when we prayed *Vouchsafe* or *Deign*,
> were creditable, sufficient to the day.

The italicized phrases carry within themselves the suspir-
ations of Catholic patience, which has lost all intention of
action. With the first, lamenting style well established,
Heaney turns to the elder generation's view of the imperious
and impervious discourse of the educated young (who had
benefited from the 1947 Education Act of the United Kingdom, giving them access to higher education):

> And next thing, suddenly, this change of mood.
> Books open in the newly-wired kitchens.
> Young heads that might have dozed a life away
> against the flanks of milking cows were busy
> paving and pencilling their first causeways
> across the prescribed texts. The paving stones
> of quadrangles came next and a grammar
> of imperatives, the new age of demands.

> [HL, 46]

The Roman hardness of 'paving and pencilling', 'prescribed
texts', 'the paving stones of quadrangles' matches the dis-

course of demands: these young 'intelligences / brightened and unmannerly as crowbars' have discarded the soft light of the dozing past for their electrical imperatives. As the poem continues its play on grammar the speaker, realizing the weakness of the old optatives, yet disliking the new imperatives that 'would banish the conditional for ever', stands anticipating the Deluge, yearning for one person, a new Noah, 'who stood his ground in the indicative, / whose boat will lift when the cloudburst happens' (HL, 47). Although the organization of the poem is perhaps over-schematized by its grammatical armature, its three parts – nationalist exhausted optatives, youthful imperatives and the yearning for an indicative – sketch the state of the Northern Catholic population, and its competing discourses, without ever mentioning it by name.

Although I have been drawing the allegorical back to the topical, it is time for me to return these poems to their intended genre. Generational conflict is, as 'From the Canton of Expectation' demonstrates, centrally a matter of conflicting styles; and the same can be said of cultural conflict (in which even a habit of reticence and a habit of garrulity – as Heaney tells us in 'From the Land of the Unspoken' – can cause a crucial division). Turning the material world of politics into the immaterial world of cultural habit is one of the strategies of these poems; but an equal strategy, as I have said, is Heaney's discovery of material equivalents for his virtual realms – the electric light of the unmannerly intelligence, the wooden ark of indicative integrity.

In 'Parable Island', a poem dealing with the metaphysics of naming, the poet has taken up his habitation in a place where all appellation is contested: the natives have one name for a mountain, the occupiers another; to one school of archaeologists 'the stone circles are pure symbol', to another, they are 'assembly spots or hut foundations'. There are no reliable directions in this island:

> to the solidarity I angled for,
> and played the ancient Roman with a razor.

That is Tone's first self-account. The second 'movement' of this three-movement self-elegy reflects on the ultimate collapse of the revolutionary attempt. This is the moment of parable in the poem, as Tone invents a metaphor for himself – that of a 'shouldered oar':

> I was the shouldered oar that ended up
> far from the brine and whiff of venture,
>
> like a scratching-post or a crossroads flagpole,
> out of my element among small farmers[.]

It is at this parabolic moment that the persona of Wolfe Tone and the person of Seamus Heaney converge: we feel in the lines a glimmer of Heaney in the Republic after 1972, 'far from the brine and whiff of venture, / ... out of [his] element among small farmers'. The anxieties of 'Exposure' once more show their head.

How to end such a poem? We have seen the impervious United Ireland aristocrat; we have seen the abandoned oar. With a great surprising move, the poem's third movement (again, with a debt to Lowell, this time to his 'Quaker Graveyard') plunges us into the 1796 gale that drove the sea into the French ships and sent them running, bare-masted, before the wind:

> I who once wakened to the shouts of men
> rising from the bottom of the sea,
>
> men in their shirts mounting through deep water
> when the Atlantic stove our cabin's dead lights in

and the big fleet split and Ireland dwindled
as we ran before the gale under bare poles.

[HL, 44]

The excitements of this passage – shouts and shirts, rising
and mounting, splittings and dwindlings, the bursting of
windows – climax with the flash of the 'bare poles' of the
fleeing ships set against the 'crossroads flagpole' of the rusti-
cated life. The preterite 'I . . . wakened' of the recollected
storm is asserted against both the imperfect tenses of habit
('I affected . . . I was') and the matching suicidal preterite
('[I] played the ancient Roman'). The two preterites mark
the two significant accomplishments of Tone's life – his
active sea-venture and his 'Roman' suicide.

Of Tone's three successive self-portraits – the initial crisp
account of his pre-revolutionary life and his post-
revolutionary suicide; the morose middle metaphor of his
inter-revolutionary inactivity; and the wild rousing moment
of his first sea-attack – the defining one remains the third.
Here he abandons the aloof hauteur of his first narration
and the second's moody self-distancing as a displaced oar;
he moves instead into a moment of sheer aliveness, of terror
and exaltation combined. There the fundamental nature of
the revolutionary temperament announces itself – as one
which loves action, perhaps, more than either cause or
nation.

A poem such as 'Wolfe Tone', though reaching back to
a historical personage and to the complex historical events
of the Irish 1790s, refines both personage and events into
a few bold strokes, out of which it makes a telling triptych.
On the left, we see the cockade and the razor, like a saint's
attributes; in the middle, we are shown the oar, a symbol;
and to the right, we face the gale. Considered in this light,
'Wolfe Tone' resembles a parable like 'From the Frontier

of Writing', where we saw the perfect diptych: on the left, the political frontier; on the right, the frontier of writing. And we can see a resemblance to both in 'From the Canton of Expectation', again a triptych: on the left, the pious optatives; in the middle, the defiant imperatives; on the right, the sturdy indicative.

I do not mean to take anything away from these accomplished poems by reducing them to their armatures as diptychs or triptychs. (I take warrant for the pictorial analogy from Heaney's 'Triptych' in *Field Work*.) I simply want to show how Heaney's clarity of structure, as it is schematized into such geometric forms, allies itself well with the poet's attention to the invisible realms of conscience, consciousness and language.

It is language that underpins 'Alphabets', the touching opening poem of *The Haw Lantern*, which narrates (in sixteen third-person heroic quatrains) the growth of the poet's mind and sensibility as he internalizes successive languages: English, Latin, Irish and Greek. The charm of the narration lies in the protagonist's passage from naive child-language to the self-conscious but also expansive buoyancy of adult expression. In part I (the shortest) the child learns to write numbers and letters, and feels the first stirrings of the metaphorical:

> A swan's neck and swan's back
> Make the 2 he can see now as well as say . . .

> There is a right
> Way to hold the pen and a wrong way . . .

> A globe in the window tilts like a coloured O.

In Part II the boy learns Latin; to this is added Irish with its uncial script (awakening both the Muse and the sexual

instinct in her 'tenebrous thickets'). The youthful poet is
also schooled in ascetic religion:

> Book One of *Elementa Latina*,
> Marbled and minatory, rose up in him . . .
>
> He left the Latin forum for the shade
>
> Of new calligraphy that felt like home . . .
> The lines of script like briars coiled in ditches.
>
> Here in her snooded garment and bare feet,
> All ringleted in assonance and woodnotes,
> The poet's dream stole over him like sunlight
> And passed into the tenebrous thickets . . .
>
> Christ's sickle has been in the undergrowth.
> The script grows bare and Merovingian.

In part III we learn that the boy's childhood school has
been bulldozed for new development, and with the sale of
his family's farm the Greek deltas of potato drills, the
lambdas of stooks at harvest and the omegas of good-luck
horseshoes have disappeared. The boy himself, now adult,
has come to the other side of the globe and is a university
lecturer, has entered the sphere where the extensions of
knowledge are infinite. Yet, spurred by the example of a
Renaissance necromancer (Marsilio Ficino) who wanted to
keep the whole universe in mind, and 'not just single things',
the poet aims at a wider understanding:

> The globe has spun. He stands in a wooden O.
> He alludes to Shakespeare. He alludes to Graves.
> Time has bulldozed the school and the school window,
> Balers drop bales like printouts where stooked sheaves

Made lambdas on the stubble once at harvest . . .

Yet shape-note language, absolute on air . . .
Can still command him; or the necromancer

Who would hang from the domed ceiling of his house
A figure of the world with colours in it
So that the figure of the universe
And 'not just single things' would meet his sight

When he walked abroad.

Finally, the poet desires the matchlessly comprehensive
vision of the astronaut beholding 'The risen, aqueous, singular, lucent O' – and (coming full circle to the original child,
but now in the first person) compares that grand extraterrestrial view to his own astonished realization of the miraculous
fit between letters and meanings, recalling

My own wide pre-reflective stare
All agog at the plasterer on his ladder
Skimming our gable and writing our name there
With his trowel point, letter by strange letter.

[HL, 1–3]

Though 'Alphabets' (which was composed as a Phi Beta
Kappa poem for Harvard) is specific in summoning up many
material facts of Heaney's life – a rural origin, Catholic
secondary schooling, the profession of teacher and a necromancer encountered in his reading – Heaney nowhere says
'Mossbawn', 'St Columb's', 'Harvard' or 'Ficino'. (The
mention that it was the Emperor Constantine who saw a
'sky-lettered IN HOC SIGNO' is the exception to the
anonymity of reference, since the naming of the Emperor

is necessary to fix Heaney's historical allusion to the apotheosis of writing by God himself.) Just as the astronaut 'sees all he has sprung from' as a 'singular, lucent O', so the poet will see his world without proper names or limiting geographical identification. To this extent, 'Alphabets' co-operates in the abstracting motive of *The Haw Lantern*. The volume's point of view is just far enough removed from identifying the soldiers at the road-block, or the exact nationalist rituals in 'From the Canton of Expectation', or the schoolhouse in 'Alphabets' to make it 'impossible' (as it would be for the 'astronaut') to say just where on earth this road-block or this ritual or this 'wooden O' is located. They are everywhere – so the volume implies – and here. A diffuse and yet specific mode of description, consequent upon a removed 'astronaut's' view, is Heaney's principal strategy in this parabolic mode, in which the concepts of 'emptiness', 'neutrality' and 'space' take on central imaginative importance.

Second Thoughts

What happens – after *The Haw Lantern* – to the empty space, the realm of the virtual, the geometric structures and the genre of parable? One answer is that they generate Heaney's 'squarings' – poems of four pentameter tercets in *Seeing Things* – which will occupy the next chapter. Another answer can be found in the enigmatic, teasing poem 'The Thimble' in *The Spirit Level*. 'The Thimble' is parabolic, but in historical close-up. It argues that every object is (as we might say today) an 'absent centre' around which every culture weaves a different text of meaning. So the way to 'read' universally, Heaney now proposes, is not to take the far-removed extraterrestrial view which makes every country have the same generalized road-block or the same elegiac rituals; rather, one should 'read' universally by seeing how one specific object is differently elaborated through times and cultures. What is kept constant is no longer (as in parabolic form) the empty or the universalized; the constant is the concrete object, meandering from one adaptation to another. Heaney's chosen object, the thimble – which begins (1) in Pompeii as a container for a painter's 'special red', good for making erotic bite-marks on his carnal frescoes – migrates thence into (2) a monastic relic of St Adaman: although it was once a bell – according to the credulous medieval legend – it was by a miracle shrunk into 'Adaman's Thimble'. It passes briefly (3) through the child-poet's mind as an evocative word, as Heaney invokes 'mention' – the first sign of linguistic consciousness – rather than functional 'use':

> Was this the measure of the sweetest promise,
> The dipped thirst-brush, the dew of paradise
> That would flee my tongue when they said 'A
>   thimbleful'?

And now? In current punk culture, what does the thimble become?

4

> Now a teenager
> With shaved head
> And translucent shoulders
> Wears it for a nipple-cap.

What next? The poet can't guess, but is certain that the post-millennium culture will find something interesting to do with the thimble, too:

5

And so on.

[SL, 42–3]

This *jeu d'esprit* suggests that what would scandalize the pious monks (Pompeii's House of Carnal Murals) might be right in tune with the postmodern teenager; and what the poet sighs for imaginatively ('the dew of paradise') may not be far from the medieval monk's credulity; and the 'dew of paradise' itself may not be remote from the teenager's 'translucent' shoulders. Through all the revolutions of culture, the thimble has come in handy; and will for ever. The love of the close-up was bound to reassert itself in Heaney after his engagement with the distant view; and it does so, with an almost flirtatious revenge, in 'The Thimble'.

6

Airiness:
Seeing Things

Focused and drawn in by what barred the way.
'Field of Vision' (ST, 22)

If the imaginative importance of a non-phenomenal place
'utterly empty, utterly a source' ('Station Island' III; 'Clearances' 8) was Heaney's point of origin for *The Haw Lantern*,
then a strange new return to the phenomenal world – but
from an almost posthumous perspective – is the point of
origin for *Seeing Things*. In the theory-poem of the volume
(which retells a story taken from the Irish annals) the transcendent and the real become defined as the obverse and
reverse of a single perception. Just as an angel's world would
seem miraculous to us, so our world would seem miraculous
to a heavenly person – it would, for him, represent the
wholly other, the imagined, the hitherto-inconceivable. Can
we, as human beings, begin to think of our phenomenal
surroundings in this way – as a continuing revelation of the
miraculous? This is to reverse the religious practice of 'lifting up' one's eyes to an idealized and transcendent space;
it is to find ultimate value in what we can here behold. The
poem 'The annals say' is number viii of Heaney's forty-
eight-poem sequence called 'Squarings' (poems 'square' in
shape, five beats wide and twelves lines long):

The annals say: when the monks of Clonmacnoise
Were all at prayers inside the oratory
A ship appeared above them in the air.

The anchor dragged along behind so deep
It hooked itself into the altar rails
And then, as the big hull rocked to a standstill,

A crewman shinned and grappled down the rope
And struggled to release it. But in vain.
'This man can't bear our life here and will drown,'

The abbot said, 'unless we help him.' So
They did, the freed ship sailed, and the man climbed
    back
Out of the marvellous as he had known it.

[ST, 62]

The poem's two realms represent (according to Heaney in his essay 'Frontiers of Writing') 'two orders of knowledge which we might call the practical and the poetic; ... the frontier between them is there for the crossing' (RP, 203). The poem implies that just as it would be death for the man from heaven to remain in the thicker air of earth, so it would be equally fatal to human beings to attempt to breathe for any length of time the rarefied air of the transcendent. We may ascend to it for a short glimpse of the marvellous, but we must then return to the phenomenal world. The same point is made by Heaney's epigraph and epilogue to *Seeing Things*: the first is his translation of *The Aeneid*'s passage on the golden bough – which allows one to pass into the Underworld and then return – and the second is his translation of Charon's refusal, in *The Inferno*, to take the living Dante into his ship of death.

Not even the vacancy of death can destroy for Heaney the beauty of uninhabited nature. His eye and ear and palate respond as ardently as ever to its sights and sounds and tastes. That is the first import of the title *Seeing Things* – re-inspecting the phenomenal world in the aftermath of death – but the second is a quasi-visionary insight, or numinous *frisson*, 'seeing things' with Wordsworthian imagination. Because landscape is for Heaney a powerful repository of memory, many 'Squarings' represent returns as a conscious adult to some scene from youth:

> Re-enter this as the adult of solitude,
> The silence-forder and the definite
> Presence you sensed withdrawing first time round.
>
> [ST, 69]

The ghostliness of the writer himself in these return-poems marks them as different from his earlier representations of childhood, 'When the whole world was a farm that eked and crowed' (ST, 32). Now, the self-consciousness of writing and the presence of death cannot be evaded or overlooked. It is for this reason that the landscapes and homescapes of 'Squarings' are 'airy' rather than 'laden', static rather than dynamic, 'distanced' rather than proximate, made to resemble stills rather than moving pictures. Early in 'Squarings' Heaney recalls how Hardy, 'at parties in renowned old age', sometimes 'imagined himself a ghost / And circulated with that new perspective' (ST, 61). The airiness of *Seeing Things* occurs because Heaney is contemplating the physical through the scrim of extinction.

That is the given of the book: What does the phenomenal world look like contemplated through eyes made intensely perceptive by unignorable annihilation? Such a given entails an alteration of style: not the rich sensuality of *Death of a*

Naturalist, not the historicized thickness of the bog poems, not the epic-derived Viking sparenesses of *North*, not the parabolic folk-quality of *The Haw Lantern*, but rather an almost Shaker simplicity of the actual. It is, however, an actual that cannot be touched: the scrim prevents touching. Nor can it be tasted, like the oysters of *Field Work*. It cannot be sexual. It depends chiefly on what used to be called the 'higher' or 'theoretical' senses of sight and hearing, those which make contact with their objects without touching them.

Heaney is concerned here with our immaterial extrapolations from the material – the physical arc of a pitchfork extended in imagination, pretended boundaries marked only by 'four jackets for four goalposts', or

> the imaginary line straight down
> A field of grazing, to be ploughed open
> From the rod stuck in one headrig to the rod
> Stuck in the other.

> [ST, 9]

These imagined grids and lines are the latitude and longitude lines (as Stevens spoke of them in 'The Idea of Order at Key West') by which mentality orders the world. They become more visible to the poet as ghostly returner than they were to him as first-time encounterer.

Of course such a self-aware book must also contain a nostalgia for first-order experience. This is most acutely felt in 'The Pulse' (part 2 of 'Three Drawings'). 'The pulse of the cast line / entering water' is evoked as the fleetest version of the tactile ('smaller in your hand / than the remembered heartbeat / of a bird'), and then to touch evanescent is added touch resistant:

> Then, after all of that
> runaway give, you were glad
>
> when you reeled in and found
> yourself strung, heel-tip
> to rod-tip, into the river's
> steady purchase and thrum.
>
> [ST, 11]

But now, by the time of *Seeing Things*, there can be no prospect of one's resumption into the unthinking thrum of the living current. It is as though a portcullis had dropped between Heaney and materiality: he sees the world, he relishes it, he responds to it – but

> He felt at one with space
>
> unroofed and obvious –
> surprised in his empty arms.
>
> [ST, 12]

'Unroofed' is in fact the word which generates the first of the 'Squarings', as the poet brilliantly abstracts – in the image of the many derelict roofless cottages found in Ireland – what it is to find oneself alone in the family house after the deaths of one's parents. Though at first the poem's shivering beggar-surrogate leads Heaney to summon up the Christian fiction of the 'particular judgement' – when one is judged, alone, exposed to the gaze of God, after death – he discards that fiction for the truth: 'there is no next-time-round'. What one is faced with in the ruined family house, says Heaney's final line, is 'Unroofed scope' ('scope' being a word of emptiness remembered from 'The Cleric' in *Sweeney Redivivus*):

Shifting brilliancies. Then winter light
In a doorway, and on the stone doorstep
A beggar shivering in silhouette.

So the particular judgement might be set:
Bare wallstead and a cold hearth rained into –
Bright puddle where the soul-free cloud-life roams.

And after the commanded journey, what?
Nothing magnificent, nothing unknown.
A gazing out from far away, alone.

And it is not particular at all,
Just old truth dawning: there is no next-time-round.
Unroofed scope. Knowledge-freshening wind.

[ST, 55]

Disturbingly antithetical terms – brilliancies, beggar; light, silhouette; bare, bright – prepare the reader for the central image of chilly reflection, which is no longer the family hearth with the warmth of first-order fire, but rather the inhuman but beautiful cloud-life reflected in the second-order puddle of reflection. One cannot deny the beauty of the free drift of the unsouled clouds, but the puddle refuses to be transparent to the spiritual. A flood of resigned negations follows – *Nothing, nothing, not, no next-time* – but is checked by 'scope' and 'wind'. 'Le vent se lève; il faut tenter de vivre,' says Valéry in 'Le Cimetière Marin', in a parallel refusal of the death-temptation.

If, earlier, Heaney's aim was to pull language as close as possible to the thing itself – so that a bog poem sounded boggy or a Viking-ship poem sounded lithe – he now contemplates an aesthetic in which the medium would be far from the thing represented. The theoretical formulation of this aesthetic appears in his title-poem 'Seeing Things', in which he describes a medieval baptism of Jesus carved in stone on the façade of a European cathedral. Nothing could be more unlike real water than the 'hard and thin and sinuous' lines that symbolize the river in which Jesus stands:

> *Claritas.* The dry-eyed Latin word
> Is perfect for the carved stone of the water
> Where Jesus stands up to his unwet knees
> And John the Baptist pours out more water
> Over his head: all this in bright sunlight
> On the façade of a cathedral. Lines
> Hard and thin and sinuous represent
> The flowing river. Down between the lines
> Little antic fish are all go. Nothing else.

Is there, the poem asks, a mode of representation which would be not literal but hieroglyphic, as the carved lines in stone are symbolic of, rather than mimetic of, liquid? If so – if the merest indices can summon up in the beholder's mind all the properties of water – then perhaps all the chiaroscuro of mimetic representation can be made to occur within a 'stony' art: for see, this is what happens as we look at the stone:

> And yet in that utter visibility
> The stone's alive with what's invisible:
> Waterweed, stirred sand-grains hurrying off,
> The shadowy, unshadowed stream itself.

The poet urges himself to trust the comparable 'utter visibility' of language – in 'lines hard and thin and sinuous' – and to believe that his reader can supply the implications. He concludes by averring that there can be – in poetry as in

Egyptian writing – a symbolic 'hieroglyph for life itself', faithful to the 'zig-zag' complexity of its object.

> All afternoon, heat wavered on the steps
> And the air we stood up to our eyes in wavered
> Like the zig-zag hieroglyph for life itself.

> [ST, 17]

Seeing Things is, then, a book of symbolic and indicative hieroglyphs – the unroofed wallstead, the carved river – rather than a representational book such as *Station Island*. Yet it draws its hieroglyphs from the material world, and does not insert them into parables in the manner of *The Haw Lantern*. It is interested in a mode of vision focused by – but not on – damage: its exemplary figure is therefore Heaney's Aunt Mary in her wheelchair, who can look only on the unchanging scene outside the house, seeing always 'The same small calves with their backs to wind and rain, / The same acre of ragwort, the same mountain'. Her uncomplaining steadfastness makes vision itself compelling, like a view focused by being barred by a gate:

> you could see

> Deeper into the country than you expected
> And discovered that the field behind the hedge
> Grew more distinctly strange as you kept standing
> Focused and drawn in by what barred the way.

> [ST, 22]

All of *Seeing Things* is 'focused and drawn in by what barred the way': the hollow of absence brings out presence, in the plainest and most explicit language. Once again we encounter 'things founded clean on their own shapes', but they are no longer shapes of primary sense experience, nor yet of second-order retrievals of memory, as in 'The Peninsula' (DD, 21), but rather shapes of third-order symbolic abstraction – as if only abstraction were strong enough to act as a counter to the annihilating force of death that erases senses and memory alike.

I should pause to say that the backlash from his venture into abstraction sends Heaney spinning into the primary materiality of dirt and sex, yet even these cannot resist the abstracting impulse. Dirt is made magical by 'Wheels within Wheels', where the child who will grow up to be the poet moves his bicycle to a mud-hole; upside down, with its saddle and handlebars submerged, it sends up by its turning wheels a shower of silt:

> The world-refreshing and immersed back wheel
> Spun lace and dirt-suds there before my eyes
> And showered me in my own regenerate clays.
> For weeks I made a nimbus of old glit.
> Then the hub jammed, rims rusted, the chain snapped.

[ST, 47]

With the terminal snapping of the chain here, and the disappearance of the 'nimbus', Heaney bids farewell to his most ambitious wish – to join the domain of mud with the domain of vision. Earlier, in *The Haw Lantern*, the parable-poem 'The Mud Vision' had projected such a conjunction, in which there appeared

> Our mud vision, as if a rose window of mud
> Had invented itself out of the glittery damp,
> A gossamer wheel, concentric with its own hub
> Of nebulous dirt, sullied yet lucent.

[HL, 48]

Although the Hamlet-word 'sullied' and the transcendent word 'lucent' strive for a balance both complementary and adversative, the spectators were not equal to the vision, and so it disappeared.

But by the time of *Seeing Things* mud has hardened from its nimbus-gaiety into a quarried cliff-face looming over water – Heaney's new hieroglyph of the world governed by the intractable laws of physical necessity. The question now is not how to reconcile the sullied flesh with the lucent soul, but how – in 'Squarings' x – to reconcile the water of the diaphanous virtual with the rock of the massive material:

> Ultimate
>
> Fathomableness, ultimate
> Stony up-againstness: could you reconcile
> What was diaphanous there with what was massive?
>
> [ST, 64]

The imagination must work to set mobility of mind against the immobility of the inhuman.

If mud cannot prevail against death, then perhaps sex can? The potent and Pan-like figure of 'the rope man', demonstrating his wares at the fair, appears (in 'Squarings' xviii) to challenge, with his virility, the tamer lives of the local farmers: in the end, they do not take up his challenge, and he must dismantle his magic. Sunset falls on the fair-day and the rope-man concedes his own ending; the free swaggerer of sex is, when last seen, emptied of his aura. The poem that began with the 'foul-mouthed god of hemp come down to rut' ends with 'his powerlessness once the fair-hill emptied' (ST, 74). The mud-vision, the rut-vision – both seem reprieves from despair, but they cannot be made permanent.

In *Seeing Things* almost every hieroglyph inscribes within

itself its own annihilation: 'The places I go back to have
not failed / But will not last' (ST, 101). The violence of the
Second World War is dissolved into 'newsreel bomb-hits,
as harmless as dust-puffs' (ST, 76). Even the sturdy parental
house, after the poet's father dies of cancer, becomes an
X-ray of itself, as it too takes on the quality of abstraction
into paradigm:

> The house that he had planned
> 'Plain, big, straight, ordinary, you know,'
> A paradigm of rigour and correction,
>
> Rebuke to fanciness and shrine to limit,
> Stood firmer than ever for its own idea
> Like a printed X-ray for the X-rayed body.

> [ST, 91]

In the light of such a passage, we can see that each hieroglyph
is to 'stand for its own idea', and that abstraction itself, in these
hieroglyphs, is a 'rebuke to fanciness and shrine to limit'. One
could say that the hieroglyphic poems, in their plainness of
diction (not necessarily accompanied by plainness of structure or of imagination), represent an aesthetic of which Patrick Heaney might not be ashamed. Heaney aims at 'an art
that knows its mind', 'unfussy and believable' (ST, 97).

Because *Seeing Things* is a book so pervaded by extinction,
its hieroglyphs of what remains – recreating moments of fullness of feeling – are particularly striking. The last of these
returns to 'water and ground in their extremity' (as in 'The
Peninsula' in *Door into the Dark*) and foreshadows 'Postscript'
in *The Spirit Level*, where 'the wind / And the light are working
off each other'. It too records a glittering epiphany:

> When light breaks over me
> The way it did on the road beyond Coleraine

Where wind got saltier, the sky more hurried

And silver lamé shivered on the Bann
Out in mid-channel between the pointed poles,
That day I'll be in step with what escaped me.

[ST, 108]

That elusive river light (chillier than Wordsworth's) is one
that is hoped for rather than attained. Its shiver is ecstatic
but wintry. By contrast, 'Squaring' xxiv, Heaney's hymn to
natural sufficiency, records the ever-present potential of the
senses for a fuller happiness. Although this 'Squaring' is
the single most tranquil point in *Seeing Things*, it begins,
significantly, with the word 'Deserted', making the seaside
landscape non-social. The solitary view offers nothing but
itself, an equilibrium of air and ocean. Here, the minatory
'rock' of the quarry-face ('Squarings' x) has miniaturized
itself into a little litter of hard material substances – cockles,
bottle-glass, shell-debris, a bit of sandstone. In Heaney's
wish for emblematic stillness there is almost no sound, and
no sudden flashing of light. Instead, the hieroglyphic world
simply *is*:

Deserted harbour stillness. Every stone
Clarified and dormant under water,
The harbour wall a masonry of silence.

Fullness. Shimmer. Laden high Atlantic
The moorings barely stirred in, very slight
Clucking of the swell against boat boards.

Perfected vision: cockle minarets
Consigned down there with green-slicked bottle glass,
Shell-debris and a reddened bud of sandstone.

Air and ocean known as antecedents
Of each other. In apposition with
Omnipresence, equilibrium, brim.

[ST, 80]

The sign of happiness here is Heaney's return to the
fanciful in the 'cockle minarets' and 'reddened bud of sandstone'. There is an elated elaboration of grammar as well,
as the poet suspends his perceptions on a visible string of
past participles – *deserted, clarified, perfected, consigned, known*
– and an equally visible string of concrete and abstract
nouns: *stone, wall, masonry, silence, fullness, shimmer, Atlantic,
moorings, clucking, swell, boards, vision, minarets, glass, debris,
bud, sandstone, air, ocean, antecedents, apposition, omnipresence,
equilibrium, brim*. No one could fail to notice the see-saw
between the most material nouns (*stone, boards, glass*) and
the most evanescent ones (*shimmer, equilibrium*). Even the
adjectives, in this poem of stillness, are mostly solid nouns
pressed into adjectival service: *harbour, boat, cockle, bottle,
shell*. One feels oneself to be fully in the presence of the
material harbour scene – masonry, boat, stone – and equally
in the presence of its felt aura – one of fullness, shimmer,
equilibrium. All the elements of language, too, are in balance, the Latinate 'clarified and dormant' weighing against
the Anglo-Saxon 'swell against boat boards'. In the final
sway of immaterial air against material water, each becomes
'antecedent' to the other, and neither takes priority. Air and
ocean are then placed in a further Latinate 'apposition' with
three extraordinary nouns – 'Omnipresence, equilibrium,
brim' – the first theological, the second scientific, the third
emotional. The first and second are Latinate, as befits their
learned derivation, the third Anglo-Saxon, as befits its pri-
macy of emotion: and the easy 'slippage' by which – '-brium'
drops off its Latinate 'u' and becomes the Middle-English

sensual 'brim' is the sign of ecstatic sufficiency in the present.

But – it should be said once more – this ecstatic sufficiency happens less within the flesh than within the mind: within a still and deserted moment vision is 'perfected', and air and ocean are 'known' in their reciprocity. The dynamic life of flesh would break this perfection – and so this poem of thanksgiving too is, like all 'perfected' things, a hieroglyph of death.

The anguish of the knowledge of death in *Seeing Things* is usually expressed in deliberately muted ways. But it can be seen explicitly in two 'bookends' of 'Squarings', one of which (xii) represents the good thief – whose death is imminent – and the other (xxxiv) a soldier bound for Vietnam – whose potential death makes him seem like a revenant. Though the excruciating suffering of the thief stands to be alleviated through Christ's promise – 'This day thou shalt be with me in Paradise' – it is the suffering that dominates Heaney's almost surreal description of the good thief's death-agony, as he scans 'empty space' where heaven should be:

>   paint him on Christ's right hand, on a promontory
> Scanning empty space, so body-racked he seems
> Untranslatable into the bliss
>
> Ached for at the moon-rim of his forehead,
> By nail-craters on the dark side of his brain.

> [ST, 66]

If the crucified thief stands for the intolerable knowledge of the physical pain of dying, then the bleached face of the soldier stands for what one learns on the other side of death, its emptying of human experience. Heaney saw the soldier on the airport bus in California:

The face I see that all falls short of since

Passes down an aisle: I share the bus
From San Francisco Airport into Berkeley
With one other passenger, who's dropped

At the Treasure Island military base
Half-way across Bay Bridge. Vietnam-bound,
He could have been one of the newly dead come
    back,

Unsurprisable but still disappointed,
Having to bear his farmboy self again,
His shaving cuts, his otherworldly brow.

                    [ST, 92]

So too must Heaney return to 'bear his farmboy self again',
with only his 'otherworldly brow' to mark the passage he
has undergone through his parents' deaths. Everything is
so 'normal' – the airport, the bus, the passenger being
dropped off. Yet once the dead are admitted into consciousness, the 'otherworldly brow' is the result, borne like an
uninterpretable sign – comparable to Hawthorne's minis-
ter's black veil – among one's fellows.

It was a great surprise to many of Heaney's readers –
fresh from the archaeological rites of *North*, the actual Irish
persons and contemporary events of 'Station Island' and the
political parables of *The Haw Lantern* – to come upon the
abstract, unmythologized and mostly unpolitical hieroglyphs of *Seeing Things*. The volume proves the degree to
which, for a poet, a new sense of life must generate a new
style. In 'a time marked by assent and by hiatus' (ST, 70)
– the suspended time of recognition rather than action –
the poet makes an inventory of what will bear holding on

to. 'Roof it again. Batten down. Dig in.' Instead of the
first-order quiver of sensation, or the elegiac replay of
second-order memory, he will enunciate the third-order
clarity of adult acknowledgement in language:

> Sink every impulse like a bolt. Secure
> The bastion of sensation. Do not waver
> Into language. Do not waver in it.

> [ST, 56]

Such a passage has the sternness of a vow. Yet Heaney can
re-do the airiness of the third-order symbolic in an ironic
comic mode as well:

> You are free as the lookout,

> That far-seeing joker posted high over the fog,
> Who declared by the time that he had got himself
>   down
> The actual ship had been stolen away from beneath
>   him.

> [ST, 29]

The symbolic style – by contrast to the first-order mimetic
style, or the second-order memorial style – acknowledges
in every moment that the actual ship (and even the remembered ship) has been stolen away by time. If the ship
has not been lifted up onto a symbolic plane – that is, made
into art – it will die with the death of those who remember
it. Re-imagined, however, it may last some time.

The powerful effort of re-imagining everything – not
representing it mimetically as it happened; not representing
it embalmed by memory; but representing it on an abstract
and symbolic plane that presents itself as such – this is

the strenuousness that underlies the hieroglyphs of *Seeing Things*. The virtue of such writing is that it records what is precious without tethering it to a limited personal place and a brief human lifetime. The poet sacrifices himself – as autobiographical persona, as narrator of his own era, as a person representing his class or ethnic group – in order to see things in the most basic terms of all, life symbolized and verbalized in the full knowledge of annihilation.

Almost every human being sees his parents predecease him; all adult children feel the 'unroofed' quality of that pang. Rather than dwell on violent death (as in *North* or 'Station Island'), let me, the poet says, see purely the co-presence always and everywhere of life and death 'known as antecedents / Of each other'. If the stasis, hiatus and stillness of this knowledge permeate *Seeing Things*, as they do; if spirit is in the ascendancy over matter; if speculation supervenes over certainty; then Heaney has honoured the shock and rupture of death as it deserves to be honoured. He has written a new chapter in the history of elegy, forgoing (for the most part) both the mournful conventions of lament and the transcendent conventions of apotheosis. Instead he stops time, looking for, and hoping to find, 'the portent / In each setting' (ST, 75). Yes, the poems are incidentally Irish – referring to Lough Neagh or Clonmacnoise or Coleraine or Yeats – but they are not either politically or ethnically 'Irish'. As almost posthumous poems, they reject such transient categories, which fall below (or lie above) the plane of present urgency, where the only thing that matters is the underlying law of relation between life and acknowledged death. As the Aeneas of the epigraph comes back from Hades, as the Dante of the epilogue comes back from Hell, so Heaney will come back – but not unchanged – in *The Spirit Level*.

Second Thoughts

And how does one write of primary experience again after having survived the chill of internalized extinction? One cannot forever bear one's 'otherworldly' brow; but original verdancy is not resumable. In 'The Walk' Heaney re-examines marriage as it appears under the sign of the charred. In the past there were excursions into pastoral paradises: 'Glamoured the road, the day, and him and her', with the river-bed 'Gravelly, shallowy, summery with pools'. But in the present of primary experience the picture is 'a negative this time, in dazzle-dark':

> Smudge and pallor where we make out you and me,
> The selves we struggled with and struggled out of,
> Two shades who have consumed each other's fire,
> Two flames in sunlight that can sear and singe.

Yet though husband and wife are still alive, and capable of angrily searing and singeing, they are also strangely ghost-like. Resembling the shades that speak to Dante, they 'seem like wisps of enervated air, / After-waves, feathery ether-shifts'. It is not, however, their destiny to remain static in this disembodied state: they are, to their own surprise,

> apt still to rekindle suddenly
> If we find along the way charred grass and sticks
> And an old fire-fragrance lingering on,
> Erotic woodsmoke, witchery, intrigue . . .

The inexplicable resurgence of primary first-order desire amid the exacerbations of death's third-order reflections is too primal to be analysed: it can merely be testified to. It leaves the couple 'none the wiser, just better primed / To speed the plough again and feed the flame' (SL, 63–4). Yet

the diction of the sexual – 'fragrance ... / Erotic
woodsmoke, witchery, intrigue' – has regenerated itself, one
aspect of that directly sensual '*Hosannah ex infernis*' (SL, 3)
that Heaney cannot help uttering.

7

An Afterwards:
The Spirit Level

the ladder of the future
and the past, besieger and besieged,
the treadmill of assault.

'Mycenae Lookout' (SL, 37)

A moment of political hope occurred in Northern Ireland
in September 1994, when the IRA Provisionals and the
Ulster paramilitaries agreed to a truce. At that moment
Seamus and Marie Heaney were visiting Tollund in Denmark, the site of the discovery of the Tollund Man, the first
of the bog bodies written about (in 1972) by Heaney. After
'a quarter-century of life waste and spirit waste' (CP, 24)
the weight of murder in the North seemed suddenly about
to be lifted, and the poet wrote 'Tollund'. He and his wife
could be, he thought,

footloose, at home beyond the tribe,

More scouts than strangers, ghosts who'd walked
     abroad
Unfazed by light, to make a new beginning
And make a go of it, alive and sinning,
Ourselves again, free-willed again, not bad.

[SL, 69]

Released back into light, freed into autonomy, sinners but without the strain of civil strife, they can once again be domestic and private. 'Tollund' can stand for a poem of Afterwards, marking – as do so many of the poems in *The Spirit Level* – one's response in a post-catastrophic moment. Responses can be joyous (as in 'Tollund'), mordant (as in the post-ceasefire sequence 'Mycenae Lookout'), courageously quotidian (as in the poem in praise of Heaney's brother, 'Keeping Going'), unevenly life-giving (as in the marriage-poem, 'The Walk') or potentially agonizing (as in 'St Kevin and the Blackbird'). Something huge has happened; but after that event life must be sustained. *The Spirit Level* enquires into that sustaining of life in an Afterwards.

'Tollund's' dream of peace was shattered by the resumption of violence and the uncertainty of the ceasefire; but during the time when it seemed that hostilities might finally be over, Heaney, who had been translating Sophocles' *Philoctetes* for the Field Day Theatre, turned to another Greek drama – Aeschylus' *Agamemnon* – as the basis for a tragic sequence called 'Mycenae Lookout'. The sequence takes a summary look, through the aftermath of the Trojan War, at the aftermath of Northern Ireland's quarter-century of civil conflict. The Mycenae lookout, Heaney's surrogate, is the Watchman in Agamemnon's palace. Conscious of the initiating sacrifice of Iphigenia by her father, privy to the adultery of Clytemnestra and Aegisthus during Agamemnon's absence at Troy, the Watchman is the helpless bystander at the murder of the returned Agamemnon, and the equally helpless witness to the prophecies of the raped Cassandra. He ends by foreseeing the murderous rivalry of Romulus and Remus which will give the next empire an equally bloody history. 'Mycenae Lookout' stands as the emotional centrepiece of *The Spirit Level*. It speaks from the impotent position of the ordinary citizen caught in the crossfire of civil atrocity, and it predicts the endemic resurgence of violence in culture, as well as representing culture's reiterated attempts to cleanse itself of that violence. For this reason I think of 'Mycenae Lookout' – which acts as a summary of troubles concluded – as representing an Afterwards. (The sporadic breakdowns of the ceasefire do not invalidate the political closure it symbolized.)

The other poems of *The Spirit Level* chiefly concern 'keeping going', a stoic Afterwards. This can mean the resuming of ordinary activity after social catastrophe, or merely enduring what Hopkins called, speaking of his own middle age, 'the jading and jar of the cart, / Time's tasking'. It is with these usually stoic, but sometimes even joyful pieces that I want to begin. They are grounded in the doings of every day: the poet as a child and his siblings playing 'train' on a sofa in the Heaney farmhouse; a Dutch potter making her vessels of clay; Heaney's brother Hugh tending his cows – 'keeping going' even during occasional epileptic 'turns' that give him vertigo: St Kevin standing motionless until the nest in his hand can hatch its eggs; Caedmon spending most of his time as a hardworking yardman; Heaney's mother 'steeping her swollen feet'; the blind neighbour Rosie Keenan and her hours of playing the piano; Marie Heaney's father, after the death of his wife, becoming more and more adventurous as he

> took the power mower in his stride.
> Flirted and vaunted . . .
> Learned to microwave.
>
> [SL, 60–1]

Above all, there is the poet's ancestor, a journeyman tailor who goes from house to house, stitching and ripping as he sits crosslegged, 'unopen, unmendacious, unillumined':

Does he ever question what it all amounts to

Or ever will? Or care where he lays his head?
My Lord Buddha of Banagher, the way
Is opener for your being in it.

[SL, 67-8]

This is the poetry of sitting at one's work, standing forgetful
of self in a parental protectiveness, going about perennial
motions, bearing one's blindness or one's widowerhood
without letting them sap one's vitality, and singing, like
Caedmon, in the intervals between one's duties.

Stoicism is by definition undramatic; it is the virtue of
middle age, when one's progress is at best horizontal, and
the future can hold only a decline. It is a matter of living
with and within the choices one has made (like the married
couple in 'A Walk'). And the formal beauty proper to stoicism – one of solidity, monumentality, simplification – has
seldom been celebrated (and even more seldom enacted) in
lyric. In part this has been a matter of chance: many of our
best poets died relatively young. One can find the poetry
of stoicism in Wallace Stevens, but there it is the wintry
poetry of the snow man, beholding 'nothing that is not there
and the nothing that is'. Heaney's temperament is more
sanguine than Stevens's, more social, more wedded to the
possibilities of hope and trust and mutual help.

For Heaney as a youth, the stoic person existed as solace
and example: as he says of the blind Rosie Keenan,

Being with her
Was intimate and helpful, like a cure
You didn't notice happening.

[SL, 66]

Characteristically, the poet does not say why, as a young person, he needed the help and 'cure' insensibly conveyed by Rosie Keenan's presence, but some grief in him was lightened by her serenity and her music. (He pays his childhood debt to her much later when he reads to her a poem he wrote 'with Keenan's well in it'. She says, 'I can see the sky at the bottom of it now.' It is implied that her gift to him was an analogous one: she revealed to the child the moral clear sky at the bottom of a dark place.) In writing Rosie Keenan into a sonnet – that form *par excellence* of passion, impetuousness, youth and 'high sentence' – Heaney expands the genre. It has not, historically, been a form aware of the handicapped or the impaired. Rosie Keenan is the first sonnet heroine to appear this way: 'Her hands were active and her eyes were full / Of open darkness and a watery shine' (ST, 65). Because Rosie Keenan is also a 'sweet-voiced, withdrawn musician' her stoicism can be assimilated into the withdrawnness of all artists into their art, and to the stoicism of marital fidelity; she is paired, in the poem 'At the Wellhead', with the poet's wife singing with closed eyes ('as you always do'): 'Dear shut-eyed one, dear far-voiced veteran' (ST, 65). The name 'veteran' is one proper to the stoic: though its Latin root means 'old', it has acquired the connotation of one who has had a long record of honourable service in any field.

There are really few anterior models for a way in which veteran status or stoic endurance can be formally enacted (as distinguished from semantically recounted) in poetry. How can one 'say' stoicism in form? One way is to mimic the continuing steadfastness of the stoic stance, and this is the path Heaney chooses in his beautiful double-poem of immobility in service, 'St Kevin and the Blackbird'. It consists of two twelve-line 'squarings'. The first 'squaring' is narrated from the outside; during the whole of it the saint remains unmoving in his cell, with his arms stretched out.

Since he occupies the entire descriptive space, he resembles, in his monumentality, a figure such as Cézanne's single male bather, who occupies the whole canvas. Around the motionless figure of St Kevin the narrator of the legend constructs his colloquial tale. The impression of simplicity is achieved not only by plainness of diction but also by the repetition of 'and' and of items in series. Another feature contributing to the poem's simplicity is the maintenance throughout of the present indicative until the 'must hold' of modal obligation (line 10) replaces it:

And then there was St Kevin and the blackbird.
The saint is kneeling, arms stretched out, inside
His cell, but the cell is narrow, so

One turned-up palm is out the window, stiff
As a crossbeam, when a blackbird lands
And lays in it and settles down to nest.

Kevin feels the warm eggs, the small breast, the tucked
Neat head and claws and, finding himself linked
Into the network of eternal life,

Is moved to pity: now he must hold his hand
Like a branch out in the sun and rain for weeks
Until the young are hatched and fledged and flown.

                    [SL, 20]

The poem is strung on seven 'and's: the opening one links this folk tale to all preceding ones; the next two link the blackbird to the saint; the fourth links sensation to reflection; the fifth links beneficent and malign weathers; and the sixth and seventh link the stages in the young birds' growth. There is no subordination of one item to another: they lie before us in the flat plane of medieval illustration. 'And here's another legend: St Kevin and the blackbird landing and laying and nesting; and the saint's submission to his plight; and sun and rain supervening; and the hatching and fledging and flying off of the young.' The 'and' narrative – which if it contained only its present-tense verbs, would be a story rather than an exemplum – is made moral by Kevin's pity obligating him to stoicism: 'now he *must*' remain in his excruciating position for weeks.

Heaney's use of series prolongs each moment of the narrative into something repetitive, thereby formally enacting the prolongation of pain entailed by Kevin's stoicism:

The saint is	a) *doing what?*	kneeling,
	b) *how?*	arms stretched out,
	c) *in what place?*	inside his cell,
His palm is	a) *where?*	out the window,
	b) *in what posture?*	stiff as a crossbeam,
A blackbird	a) lands	*and then?*
	b) lays	*and then?*
	c) settles down to nest.	
Kevin feels	a) the warm eggs,	*and what else?*
	b) the small breast,	*and what else?*
	c) the tucked neat head	*and what else?*
	d) and claws	

and, finding himself linked into the network of eternal life, is moved to pity.

Now he must hold his hand
    a) *how?*   like a branch
    b) *where?* b_1)   out in the sun
          b_2)   and rain
    c) *how long?*   for weeks
    d) *until when?*   the young are
          d_1)   hatched *and?*
          d_2)   and fledged *and?*
          d_3)   and flown.

Of course such arrangements come to the poet instinctively (since he has many templates of stylistic equivalence in his repertoire), but when we look to see how the endurance of Kevin is enacted and thereby made believable, it is in such forms that we find our answer.

In the second 'squaring' of the Kevin poem the speaker, in a prolonged interrogation, seeks to know Kevin's interior disposition during his long ordeal. How would stoicism enact itself inside a saint? Does he feel the agony of 'keeping going' or does he, so to speak, forget himself to marble? In this 'squaring' it is at first the repetition of the questions and the serial enumeration of the bodily parts of the saint (in an ascetic reversal of the 'blazon' of beauty) that make for the effect of unchanging stoic endurance:

And since the whole thing's imagined anyhow,
Imagine being Kevin. Which is he?
Self-forgetful or in agony all the time

From the neck on out down through his hurting
    forearms?
Are his fingers sleeping? Does he still feel his knees?
Or has the shut-eyed blank of underearth

Crept up through him? Is there distance in his head?

If we graph these questions, we can see that they arrange themselves in two columns forming an *abba* chiasmus in which agony is placed between speculations of self-forgetfulness:

SELF-FORGETFULNESS   AGONY

Which is he?

Self-forgetful?   *or* in agony all the time
                                           from neck through
                                           forearms?
                                           Are his fingers
                                           sleeping?
                                           Does he still feel his
                                           knees?

                             or

Has the blank crept up?
Is there distance in his head?

The close of the poem chooses the left-hand alternative, in which stoicism turns into something almost indistinguishable from lyric death. Kevin in his self-abnegation loses identity; he no longer remembers the object of his pity, and he forgets even language: he cannot recall the name of the river where love has placed him and in which he is now reflected:

Alone and mirrored clear in love's deep river,
'To labour and not to seek reward,' he prays,

A prayer his body makes entirely
For he has forgotten self, forgotten bird
And on the riverbank forgotten the river's name.

[SL, 20–21]

In his Nobel lecture Heaney calls Kevin someone who is 'true to life if subversive of common sense, at the intersection of natural process and the glimpsed ideal' (CP, 32). The entire altruism of Kevin in his fatherly protectiveness of the fledglings must perhaps remain only a 'glimpsed ideal' for any artist; but Heaney's persuasive powers are such that the reader, having been conducted phase by phase through the stages of Kevin's suffering and self-forgetfulness, ends by admiring the saint's devotion. The last enacting form in the poem is the threefold stoic series of two 'pray' / 'prayer's', three 'river's and three 'forgotten's. It is as though the saint's stoic metabolism, without intervention by conscious will, keeps producing these serial heartbeats and breaths: *river / prays / prayer / forgotten / forgotten / riverbank / forgotten / river.*

If one way of rendering stoic endurance visible is to monumentalize and simplify it, and prolong it into series and repetitions, another way is to place it in a polyptych with its contrastive opposites. In 'Keeping Going' we find a poem which folds together six orienting moments, all subtended by the poet's brother's present stamina. Instead of leaving Ulster for the Republic, as the poet did, his brother Hugh has stayed in the North to maintain the family farm, remaining equable through the horrors of the Troubles, and living in peace with his neighbours. The poem is in part an investigation of the qualities that go to make up that sort of emotional stamina, in part an overview of the atrocious conditions which make the stoic response an heroic one. The poet's summarizing address in the closing section of the poem says,

> My dear brother, you have good stamina.
> You stay on where it happens. Your big tractor
> Pulls up at the Diamond, you wave at people,
> You shout and laugh about the revs, you keep
> Old roads open by driving on the new ones.

And all this is both praiseworthy and characteristic of Hugh, as we know from scene 1 (representing his irrepressible good humour in youth) as he pretends – with an upside-down chair for pipes and a whitewash brush for a sporran – to be a piper, leading his young siblings on a march:

> Your pop-eyes and big cheeks nearly bursting
> With laughter, but keeping the drone going on
> Interminably, between catches of breath.

It is not only joyousness that lives on in Hugh, but also his steady devotion to the work he has been doing since his youth, as we see in scene 2, in which he and the young poet-to-be are, in the past, putting the whitewash brush/sporran to its proper use, freshly whitewashing the family cottage:

> . . . the slop of the actual job
> Of brushing walls, the watery grey
> Being lashed on in broad swatches, then drying out
> Whiter and whiter, all that worked like magic.

In the world of the poet's youth, whatever becomes dingy can be renewed by the magic of the re-whitening brush.

In scene 3 of the poem the atmosphere darkens, as the poet recalls the pre-Christian superstitions of childhood: the belief that the dead congregate after dark at the gable, the fact that Hugh broke his arm when the thorn tree (thought to have 'fairy' power) was cut down; 'the dread / When a strange bird perched for days on the byre roof'. In scene 4 moral evil (rather than the simple superstitions of scene 3) penetrates the innocence of the cottage: Macbeth and the witches and their apparitions hover in the background as the poet's mother warns her son against 'bad boys' at secondary school. Then, in scene 5, a sectarian murder – fulfilling all the previous pagan and Shakespearean intimations of nightmare and slaughter – occurs in town, leaving a whitewashed wall smeared with 'grey matter like gruel flecked with blood' from the head of the man shot to death, who had been leaning against the wall when his assassin's car, after crossing 'the Diamond', drove by. The victim's spilled blood is represented by the poet as a Virgilian libation which will 'feed' other murdered ghosts:

> ... he never moved, just pushed with all his
>   might
> Against himself, then fell past the tarred strip,
> Feeding the gutter with his copious blood.

It is that very spot of murder, 'the Diamond', that Hugh re-consecrates to ordinary use by pulling up to it in his tractor, with cheerful gestures of neighbourliness (scene 6). Heaney's use of the present tense of habit restores the everyday, the continued, the usual. It shows the overcoming – by simple naturalness – of the unnaturalness of violence:

> You stay on where it happens. Your big tractor
> Pulls up at the Diamond, you wave at people,
> You shout and laugh ...

A great deal of weight in favour of Hugh's choice of life is exerted by this habitual present of decency, exuberance and hard work: one feels Heaney's deep admiration for his brother's restoration of equanimity to everyday existence. Yet the poet also feels this resilience has limits to its power:

> You called the piper's sporrans whitewash brushes
> And then dressed up and marched us through the
>   kitchen,
> But you cannot make the dead walk or right wrong.

The city wall, smeared with blood, cannot be whitewashed as the cottage walls could be.

And the poet then adds a different picture of Hugh, suffering an epileptic 'turn' as the cows are being milked:

> I see you at the end of your tether sometimes,
> In the milking parlour, holding yourself up
> Between two cows until your turn goes past,
> Then coming to in the smell of dung again
> And wondering, is this all? As it was
> In the beginning, is now and shall be?

These are the questions Heaney also put to his journeyman-ancestor: 'Does he ever question what it all amounts to?' The individual life can matter so little in the scheme of things, that to look at it in far-focus ('as it was in the beginning . . .') can give no moral satisfaction. Instead, the poet allows Hugh to resume his habitual actions, but now (following the grammatical lead of the passage of vertigo) in the present participle of infinite extension:

> And wondering, is this all? . . .
> Then rubbing your eyes and seeing our old brush
> Up on the byre door, and keeping going.

> [SL, 10–12]

By the complexity of its six scenes – ranging from Shakespearean blood-murder spurred on by superstition, to the persistence of similar archaic superstition in Irish folk life, to the none the less cheerful ordinariness resiliently alive in that same Irish life, to sectarian assassination, to the momentary faltering of even such a stoic as Hugh – 'Keeping Going' inserts the virtue of the stoic Afterwards into multiple contemporary and past contexts. Heaney here stretches the lyric into unwonted narrative extension, to show that stoicism is not contextless like St Kevin's except when it is found in parable or exemplum. In daily life in the North it contends with a multitude of counter-forces, past and present, cultural and internal.

There is a happier side to endurance through time in *The Spirit Level*, but even in such a celebratory poem as ' "Poet's Chair" ' (named after a bronze chair by the sculptor Carolyn Mulholland) the half-organic chair – 'its straight back sprouts two bronze and leafy saplings' – which, in its urban setting, is occupied at some point by almost everyone in Dublin is imagined, in the middle scene of the poem, as part of the setting for a death-ritual:

> Next thing I see the chair in a white prison
> With Socrates sitting on it . . .
>   No tears
> And none now as the poison does its work.
>
> [SL, 46–47]

Though the third scene restores ordinary continuity, normalcy and hope (the thought 'of being here for good in every sense') the undeniable centrepiece of ' "Poet's Chair" ' is Socrates' exemplary and stoical death. Heaney's imagination must now somehow find room, in almost every poem, for a three-phase scenario showing, in turn, ordinary life, its violation by some event and its restoration by 'keeping going' afterwards.

While many poems in *The Spirit Level* represent these phases within the convention of present-day realism, Heaney's conviction that they are not limited to his own historical moment leads him to summon up mythic equivalents, such as the murder of Socrates or the events surrounding the Trojan War. I believe that Heaney allowed himself the unexampled linguistic violence in 'Mycenae Lookout' only because it seemed the political troubles might be over, and one could write *finis* – with a summary sequence – to the whole incomprehensible slaughter. 'Neighbourly murder' ('Funeral Rites') has always been incomprehensible to Heaney: though he might have been able (as he says in 'Punishment') to 'connive in civilized outrage' yet understand the 'exact and intimate' revenge of the Catholics who shaved the heads of girls who fraternized with British soldiers, he is unable to understand, or empathize with, the act of murder. He can at most, as in 'Mycenae Lookout', recognize its inexplicable, but apparently unstoppable recurrence in human affairs.

The five parts of 'Mycenae Lookout' are all spoken by the Watchman, whose imagination – as he waits for Agamemnon's return from Troy – has been polluted by the bloodthirstiness of the Trojan war:

> I'd dream of blood in bright webs in a ford,
> Of bodies raining down like tattered meat
> On top of me asleep.
>
> [SL, 29]

(Heaney has spoken of a comparable dream, in which he saw a bloodied man falling towards him.) By writing the Watchman's first narrative in the run-on pentameter couplets we associate with Keats's hopeful pastorals ('Sleep and Poetry', 'Endymion'), Heaney makes a sardonic 'black mirror' (SL, 30) out of what was originally a mild English narrative form. And by writing his portrait of Cassandra in the shortest possible lines (monometer, dimeter), cutting off each line almost before it has begun, he makes it savagely in tune with the abduction and abuse of the raped girl whom Agamemnon has brought back from Troy. 'No such thing,' says the Watchman, 'as innocent bystanding':

No such thing
as innocent
bystanding.

Her soiled vest,
her little breasts,
her clipped, devast-

ated, scabbed
punk head,
the char-eyed

famine gawk –
she looked
camp-fucked

and simple.

Heaney has never before permitted himself such brutal
strokes in delineating a victim. Cassandra has not been distanced by archaism (as the bog bodies were, bronzed and
stylized by quasi-petrifaction); she stands before us, through
the Watchman's eyes, as she might have been, defensive
and defenceless. Agamemnon, killer of his own daughter, is
equally violently sketched upon his return, a terrorist care-
less of the results of his will:

Old King Cock-
of-the-Walk
was back,

King Kill-
the-Child-
and-Take

What-Comes,
King Agamem-
non's drum-

balled, old buck's
stride was back.

Cassandra's prophecy – her 'bleat of clair- / voyant dread'
– merely awakes in the non-innocent 'bystanders' a wish to
rape her again:

And a result-

ant shock desire
in bystanders
to do it to her

there and then.
Little rent
cunt of their guilt.

The whole bloody crisis of the king's return, as Clytemnestra and Aegisthus throw a net over Agamemnon in the
bath and stab both him and Cassandra, takes on the language
of cartoon:

Little rent
cunt of their guilt:

in she went
to the knife,
to the killer wife,

to the net over
her and her slaver,
the Troy reaver.

Borrowing from Aeschylus, Heaney gives Cassandra the last, truncated word of this merciless poem, and she uses it to pronounce the irrationality of historical event. Unpredictably, some epochs are suffused with light, others with darkness; what is certain is that each is erased, after its fated time, by 'A wipe / of the sponge':

> in she went . . .
>
> saying, 'A wipe
> of the sponge,
> that's it.
>
> The shadow-hinge
> swings unpredict-
> ably and the light's
>
> blanked out.'
>
> [SL, 30–33]

The darkness, as chaos falls on an epoch, is signified by the two missing lines of Cassandra's last tercet.

'I felt,' says the Watchman in his dawn-vision, 'the beating of the huge time-wound / We lived inside.' And though he bends to touch the flowers with their 'pre-dawn gossamers', his soul 'wept in [his] hand', contaminating even the most innocent action with the stain of tragedy. His dawn-vision reaches forward to Romulus and Remus, to the erotic excitement of conflict, as he sees the fratricide

> a hilly, ominous place,
>
> Small crowds of people watching as a man
> Jumped a fresh earth-wall and another ran
> Amorously, it seemed, to strike him down.
>
> [SL, 34]

Heaney's rhyming triplets in this section of 'Mycenae Look-out' suggest that once something has begun ('a man'), a consequence follows as if by consonance ('another ran'); and that a chiming result ('to strike him down') is equally, and fatedly, impelled by the momentum of the first two. It is this irresistible momentum that drives the Watchman – confidant of both Clytemnestra and Agamemnon, witness of child-murder, criminal sexuality, brutal battle and regicide – to a coarseness of language that fits his tale:

> The war put all men mad,
> horned, horsed or roof-posted,
> the boasting and the bested.

[SL, 36]

Finally, in his concluding 'reverie of water', the Watchman is both doom-laden and hopeful, as though Heaney cannot rid himself of the tragic conviction that each hiatus from violence is only that – a hiatus; and yet at the same time cannot resist a trust that blood-shedding can find water for its purification. The tragic reverie shows humanity caught on

> the ladder of the future
> and the past, besieger and besieged,
> the treadmill of assault.

By contrast, the sequence ends on the sinking of a new well-shaft by men at peace,

> like discharged soldiers testing the safe ground,

> finders, keepers, seers of fresh water
> in the bountiful round mouths of iron pumps
> and gushing taps.

[SL, 37]

Heaney-the-Watchman has returned to the pump at
Mossbawn, described in *Preoccupations* as the centre, the
omphalos, of the child's world:

> There the pump stands, a slender, iron idol,
> snouted, helmeted . . . I remember . . . men coming
> to sink the shaft of the pump . . . That pump marked
> an original descent into earth, sand, gravel, water.
> It centred and staked the imagination, made its
> foundation the foundation of the *omphalos* itself.
>
> [P, 17, 20]

If water, instead of blood gushing from a 'time-wound', can
once again be made the symbol of Ireland, then hope can
return. Heaney's wish for a benign Afterwards, and his Lark-
inesque praise of water, outstrips, perhaps, any historical
foundation: but the alternative to the wish is a despair which
he finds it his moral obligation to resist.

Second Thoughts

The poet does allow despair to close one poem: 'A Dog
Was Crying Tonight in Wicklow Also' (written in memory
of a Nigerian friend, Donatus Nwoga). In the African fable
retold by the poem the god Chukwu is lied to by a toad,
who tells him that 'Human beings want death to last forever'; Chukwu so ordains. The poem ends with Heaney's
bleakest Afterwards, a tableau of annihilation and elegy:

> Great chiefs and great loves
> In obliterated light, the toad in mud,
> The dog crying out all night behind the corpse house.
>
> [SL, 56]

It is because Heaney knows both sides of the contest of matter and spirit – annihilation countered by stoicism, the virtual extinguished by the physical – that his poems have increasingly needed to be sequences, long enough and various enough – like 'Mycenae Lookout' or 'Keeping Going' or the six-part 'The Flight Path' – to embrace his sense of the undeniably contradictory aspects of experience. His steady incorporation of his past into his present, and of first thoughts into second thoughts, makes the task of truth-telling harder, and the finding of language more arduous, with each decade. Heaney has been forced, by the place and time into which he was born, to take on, within the essentially private genre to which he was called, the representation of an unignorable social dimension.

It should be remembered that the only thing to which the genre of the lyric obliges its poet is to represent his own situation and his responses to it in adequate imaginative language. Since even his most strenuous critics never seem to doubt that Heaney has shown them how he sees his situation and how his feelings respond to it, they – even in arguing against what they take to be his views – are the best witnesses to his imaginative success. Their demand that he see predicaments of politics or gender as they would, or have the same feelings about them as they do is, of course, unanswerable; that is not a demand one can make of art.

NOTES

BIBLIOGRAPHY

INDEX

NOTES

1. The most circumstantial account of Heaney's life in print is to be found in Michael Parker, *Seamus Heaney: The Making of the Poet* (London: Macmillan, 1993). In referring to Londonderry/Derry, I have followed Heaney's own usage, and used 'Derry.'

2. Letter to John Taylor, 30 January 1818; in Robert Gittings, *Letters of John Keats* (New York: Oxford, 1970), p. 59.

3. In P. J. Drudy, ed., *Irish Studies*, 1 (Cambridge: Cambridge University Press, 1980), pp. 1-20; this is from p. 14.

4. Seamus Heaney, interviewed by Brian Donnelly, in Broadridge, ed., *Seamus Heaney* (Copenhagen: Denmarks Radio, 1977), p. 60; quoted in Parker, *Seamus Heaney*, p. 105.

5. Broadridge, p. 48.

6. W. K. C. Guthrie, *The Greeks and Their Gods* (Boston: Beacon Press, 1962; reprint of 1955 corrected edition from original edition of 1952), p. 88.

7. 'A tale of two islands: reflections on the Irish Literary Revival', in Drudy, ed., *Irish Studies*, 1, pp. 1-20; this quotation is from p. 9.

8. Spenser, *A View*, quoted in *Preoccupations*, p. 34. Parker (*Seamus Heaney*, pp. 95-6), correcting from Spenser's original, substitutes 'bear' for 'carry', and omits 'like' before 'anatomies'.

BIBLIOGRAPHY

A. Works by Seamus Heaney

All, unless noted otherwise, were published in London by Faber & Faber (in the year noted) and in New York by Farrar, Straus and Giroux. For the most recent bibliography of uncollected articles, interviews and radio broadcasts by Heaney, and of criticism on Heaney and on Irish poetry, see Michael Parker, *Seamus Heaney: The Making of the Poet* (Macmillan, 1993). A complete bibliography of Heaney's work is in preparation by Randy Brandes of Lenoir-Rhyne University in the United States.

1. POETRY

Death of a Naturalist (1966)
Door into the Dark (1969)
Wintering Out (1972)
North (1975)
Field Work (1979)
And Open Letter (Derry: Field Day Theatre Company, 1983)
Station Island (1984)
Sweeney Astray (1984)
The Haw Lantern (1987)
Selected Poems 1966–1987 (1990)
Seeing Things (1991)
The Spirit Level (1996)

2. CRITICISM

Preoccupations: Selected Prose 1968–1978 (1980)
The Government of the Tongue (1988)
The Place of Writing (Atlanta: Scholars Press, 1989)
The Redress of Poetry (1995)
Crediting Poetry (the Nobel Lecture) (1996)

3. PLAYS

The Cure at Troy: A Version of Sophocles' Philoctetes (1990)

4. DISCOGRAPHY

The Northern Muse – with John Montague (Claddagh
   Records, 1968; out of print)
Seamus Heaney (Harvard University, 1987)
Stepping Stones: Selected Poems (Penguin Audio Books, 1995)
The Spirit Level (Penguin Audio Books, 1996)
Station Island (Penguin Audio Books, 1997)

B. Selected books and edited collections on Seamus Heaney

Agenda: Seamus Heaney Birthday Issue, ed. William Cookson and
   Peter Dale (London: Agenda and Editions Charitable Trust,
   1989)
Allen, Michael, ed., *Seamus Heaney: New Casebook Series*
   (London: Macmillan, 1997)
Andrews, Elmer, *The Poetry of Seamus Heaney: All the Realms of
   Whisper* (London: Macmillan, 1988)
Andrews, Elmer, ed., *Seamus Heaney: A Collection of Critical
   Essays* (London: Macmillan, 1992)
Bloom, Harold, ed., *Seamus Heaney: Modern Critical Views* (New
   York: Chelsea House, 1986)
Burris, Sidney, *The Poetry of Resistance: Seamus Heaney and the
   Pastoral Tradition* (Athens, GA: Ohio University Press, 1990)
Buttel, Robert, *Seamus Heaney* (Lewisburg: Bucknell University
   Press, 1975)
Corcoran, Neil, *Seamus Heaney* (London: Faber, 1986)
Curtis, Tony, ed., *The Art of Seamus Heaney*, revised edn.
   (Bridgend: Poetry Wales Press, 1994)
Foster, John Wilson, *The Achievement of Seamus Heaney* (Dublin:
   The Lilliput Press, 1995)
Foster, Thomas C., *Seamus Heaney* (Dublin: The O'Brien Press,
   1989)
Hart, Henry, *Seamus Heaney: Poet of Contrary Progressions* (New
   York: Syracuse University Press, 1992)
Haviaras, Stratis, ed., *Seamus Heaney: A Celebration*. A Harvard

Review Monograph (Cambridge, Mass.: The President and
Fellows of Harvard College, 1996)

Morrison, Blake, *Seamus Heaney* (London: Methuen, 1982)

Murphy, Andrew, *Seamus Heaney* (Plymouth: Northcote House,
1996)

O'Donoghue, Bernard, *Seamus Heaney and the Language of Poetry*
(New York: Harvester Wheatsheaf, 1994)

Parker, Michael, *Seamus Heaney: The Making of the Poet* (Dublin:
Gill & Macmillan, 1993)

Tamplin, Ronald, *Seamus Heaney* (Milton Keynes: Open
University Press, 1989)

INDEX